WEALTHCARE

WEALTHCARE

Demystifying Web3 and the Rise
of Personal Data Economies

BRIGITTE PINIEWSKI, MD

HOUNDSTOOTH
PRESS

WEALTHCARE

Demystifying Web3 and the Rise of Personal Data Economies

FIRST EDITION

ISBN 978-1-5445-3770-2 *Hardcover*
      978-1-5445-3771-9 *Paperback*
      978-1-5445-3772-6 *Ebook*

This book is dedicated to the individuals who are providing capital, creativity, and code to advance web3 and our aspirational ownership economy. A special callout to developers, sometimes underappreciated and undercompensated: you're the unsung heroes of our preferred tomorrow.

CONTENTS

PART V: PUSHING THROUGH PUSHBACK

INTRODUCTION

Every system is perfectly designed to get the results it gets.
—The W. Edwards Deming Institute

Before jumping into the complexities of web3 tech, let's start with an example that is increasingly familiar.

For Troy, puberty did not go as planned. He carried extra weight into his teens, and the fallout of those years is significant. Now in his mid twenties, his physique is an unexpected blend of male and female: he carries prominent breast tissue, an abdominal fat pad, and another fat pad above his pubis. Below his pubic fat pad are uncharacteristically small sex organs, almost as if his genitals remain arrested in the toddler stage. He's embarrassed to take his shirt off in front of others because of the shape of his chest and midline, and group showering is out of the question.

Here's what we know: most domains of human functioning can be significantly—and sadly, irreversibly—impaired through an ill-fated four years of puberty, a time when we're all much too young to know what is happening to us, let alone how it's meant to shape our futures. In boys, this flood of hormonal messaging starts roughly around age eleven or twelve, when many boys today are carrying around excess weight: ten, twenty, even fifty pounds. Unknown to most children and families is that these extra fat cells may be creating and secreting hormones of their own.

A little extra hormonal secretion may be without consequence, but when sufficiently extra amounts of hormone are present, they can block intended messaging to receptors throughout the body (e.g. skin, hair, muscles, sex organs, central nervous system). One of these fat-cell-derived hormones is estrone, a female sex hormone, which can wreak havoc on a body expecting overwhelming testosterone-rich messaging.

In some cases, like Troy's, these young men develop more prominent breast and abdominal fat tissue. Remarkably, men also can experience stretch marks on their outsized breasts and abdomen. Meanwhile, their reproductive anatomy may remain remarkably underdeveloped, small in size and shape. Brains, bones, skin, and muscles may all develop according to a mixed hormonal messaging. This cascade of disordered puberty can have physical, mental, and social outcomes that their parents do not anticipate and that the child, now grown, is unprepared for.

Troy's pubertal mishap occurred without his or his parents' knowledge or consent. Did Troy's doctor know? Perhaps not. Many children may not visit their physicians as they are not sharing their development, or lack thereof, with their parents.

Waiting to intervene after any child is already carrying excessive weight can be remarkably difficult. Kids are reluctant to change, and parents don't want to cause eating disorders or other pathologies. They hope their child will "grow out of it." It is difficult to blame healthcare that isn't built to manage the ebb and flow of insulin resistance in children, much less the minutiae of day-to-day co-occurrences that collectively result in these unexpected outcomes. Still, if healthcare isn't to blame, then who is?

Troy's parents, while well educated, were ill-equipped to understand the ramifications of what was happening. They had no streams of data on which they could rely and no collective insight into what the future might look like for their son. They had no idea where to find a game plan that other teens and families had followed through similar situations.

ACCIDENTAL WELLNESS IS A THING OF THE PAST

As a frontline physician and medical executive for many years, I have witnessed firsthand how Troy and other individuals fare within the crosshairs of financial, educational, healthcare, and other systems. Because I'd spent many days completing full physicals on young people, especially between the ages of eighteen and twenty-four, it became clear that our medical model was not keeping up with the times.

Prior to this practice, I had assumed that it took decades of suboptimal lifestyles to generate diabetes, heart disease, and stroke. Yet I found many of the youngsters I saw were overweight or obese. I saw that, in just four years of an inappropriate maturation through puberty, it is possible to launch into premature chronic diseases of aging—not by weeks or months, but by decades.

Past generations enjoyed a certain level of accidental wellness because they relied on farm foods and activity-based employment. Granted, many from earlier generations partook in lifestyle choices that we now consider unhealthy or downright risky (e.g. smoking, abusing alcohol, not wearing seat belts), but for members of earlier generations, the chronic diseases of aging occurred much later in life.

Our traditional healthcare system was designed for those generations, and it operated as *sick care*, not *health care*—do nothing until you experience an illness or injury, and then get the care you need. Barring an acute illness, populations remain on standby, waiting to be told when to be screened, where to get vaccinations, what clinics to visit, which specialists to see, and so on.

This has worked decently enough for decades, and populations have largely remained well between episodes of illness. In this model, the *well* majority is expected to support the *unwell* minority, while diverse populations continue to expect reasonable health throughout their lives. However, the last few decades have turned these assumptions on their head, and the implications of this change are huge.

Today, we expect to have full access to our genetic potential and decent health throughout our lives, yet the defaults of cheap, convenient factory food alongside knowledge-based employment are reshaping access to our own genetic potential. Our biology expects conditions that were present centuries ago. It has no idea that we carry smartphones or stare at screens for hours. The conditions our biology expects (e.g. nutrition, sleep, activity) have been profoundly altered. Automation threatens employment; our social fabric has moved to the screen; the "upright human" now sits hunched over the phone, sending emojis in place of actually feeling emotions; social media has affected national elections.

Changes to the way we work, live, and move have ensured that newer generations are remarkably less physically well. The pace of change in our environment is problematic for our outdated biology. All told, no generation will be accidentally well again.

AVERAGE IS NOT OPTIMAL

From misaligned sex steroids during puberty to early chronic diseases of aging, the challenges ahead are immense. Every four years, another young cohort transitions through their early teens, but this hormonally sensitive period has seen some alarming adjustments in recent decades.[1] The fallout will be far reaching, and is already becoming so, with noticeable reductions in cognitive capacity, employability, and socialization.[2] The nation's competitive advantage may not survive a widespread downward spiral of human potential while other nations remain more protected from our Western lifestyle.

Rising healthcare costs also work against our competitive advantage. As Warren Buffett famously said, "medical costs are the tapeworm of American economic competitiveness."[3] As Americans, we're nothing if not competitive, yet it is no secret that US car manufacturers are paying more for healthcare than they do for steel.[4] As politicians find new ways to reduce taxes for corporations, the real financial drain is right there on the balance sheet: the employee healthcare bill, which can be three-times larger than the tax bill.

Yes, the perfect storm has been brewing for years; now it's gathering momentum. Sadly for those who don't want change, transformation is in the works.

What's behind the pending shift? As we'll discuss in this book, we are facing more than just the arrival of web3, the latest evolution of the internet. We also find ourselves in the eye of a perfect storm that includes the end of accidental wellness; COVID-19 tailwinds; privacy legislation; technology developments, including artificial intelligence, blockchain, crypto, and NFTs; and the ongoing interest in health from technology companies. These are indeed tumultuous times that make the job of fixing this multisegmented problem even more daunting.

It is a problem for the nation and for individuals like Troy, who are missing out on their physical, social, and educational potential, with little hope of maximizing their future earning arc. In fact, Troy may be the new average, and, as Dr. Eric Topol shows in the book *The Creative Destruction of Medicine*, medicine has always offered average to everyone.

In *The Creative Destruction of Medicine*, Dr. Topol details the way in which medical knowledge is based on populations but applied to individuals.[5] If you're a person living with a certain disease, you're expected to achieve the average life span and average health of a person living with said disease. But average is not ideal.

Who wants average? How can we instead achieve optimal results? Where else in our lives do we accept *average* and stop striving for *optimal*?

In order to achieve more—to provide a definition of what is

reachable—we need the benefit of the many: insight from individuals that went before us to define what is in fact within the realm of the possible. Indeed, one of the core tenets of this book is the fact that rugged individualism, celebrated or otherwise, is a myth that we as a society have outgrown.[6]

Instead, our future potential relies on timely access to the truths experienced by others. The health expression of large collectives harbors the biological truths that define what is reachable for each of us. Gaining a new high-fidelity view of human health expression will be especially valuable in the future, as the planet continues to warm, jobs continue to go toward automation, and humans across the globe continue to search for meaning, gainful employment, and ways to connect with like-minded tribes. Ultimately, should we make the leap to Mars—as some have suggested—we will need a robust collective knowledge generator that informs us at the pace of change.

OUR TECHNOLOGICAL PARADOX

We find ourselves at the nexus of a technology paradox: as technology advances, our basic biology is stymied. Yet technology also offers opportunities. Non-healthcare players have begun entering the healthcare arena, such as the FAANG group of retailers, which includes Meta Platforms (Facebook), Amazon, Apple, Netflix, and Alphabet (Google).

These companies have contributed to a world in which we do not simply rely on human brains that are capable of coordinating relatively few facts at a time. We have machines that manage millions of data points without missing a single item. We have tools such as artificial intelligence (AI) and machine learning

(ML) to uncover and coordinate relationships across a sea of data. These machines and tools are on an uninterruptible path and are getting more powerful with each passing year.

However, these tools are not without their rough patches. Not all deployments are a glossy success. Instead, our data power asymmetry expands; knowledge asymmetry expands, while our personal agency erodes. Yet hope for meaningful course correction is spreading. Many expect an expanding web3 ownership economy to reset the asymmetries of the past.

Web1 refers to the early days of the internet, a read-only online experience. Over time, the internet has changed, and so have we. The desktop became the laptop, then the tablet. The flip phone is long gone. *Plugging in* became *connecting*, *clicking* turned into *tapping*, *surfing* is now *scrolling*. Eventually, web1 gave way to our now ubiquitous web2, which goes beyond read-only to support transactions.

We shop, bank, connect, and work from just about anywhere with a wireless connection. Web2 consumes our content and data as we, all too easily, post photos and comments to social media pages in an addictive frenzy. This web2 dark side is becoming increasingly clear as we suffer the onslaught of targeted pop-up ads and bad actors blurring the boundaries of truth and fake news.

As centralized web2 services continue to aggregate and control the vast majority of our data, we as consumers remain in the dark when it comes to how these systems actually use our information. What's more, we lack meaningful incentives to engage in data ownership or data economies.

Shoshana Zuboff warned us of the perils of surveillance capitalism,[7] and Netflix's *The Social Dilemma* gathered ex-FAANG executives to explain the ubiquitous practice of unfettered data consumption as the basis for robust business models.[8] As of this writing, Mark Zuckerberg's Meta Platforms is under such a level of scrutiny that the company has pinned its hope for survival on a complete rebrand. What has become increasingly clear is that executives knowingly use data and AI to drive behaviors and drive profits. Period.

Elsewhere, Google is pushing back efforts to kill third-party cookies.[9] While this is happening, we're casting doubts on the promise of AI. A recent piece in *Wired* cited a review of 150 papers regarding the use of AI and machine learning to predict diagnosis and course of disease.[10] Sadly, the AI-based results proved remarkably problematic.

Currently, there is no easy fix. Often, both the data and the algorithms are closed; thus, other researchers are unable to check results. Additionally, the IBM Watson fire sale, as we will explore later, also suggests several reasons why these AI approaches are inherently limited.

Furthermore, in an article in the *Atlantic* called "Why Technology Favors Tyranny," Yuval Noah Harari spoke about a growing class of irrelevant or surplus populations.[11] Are we generating a new *lost class* as we automate jobs away from human workers? Are future populations at increased risk of irrelevance? This certainly seems to be true.

Have we gone too far? Can a shift to web3 offer the chance for a technological model that would re-decentralize the web, return agency to individuals, and make it easy to participate in, personally own, and manage digital assets within direct peer-to-peer transactions? An old adage says, "Life is full of unintended consequences; our futures are hard to predict." Should we take advantage of a robust web3 future, plus enlist AI and ML expansion, in the quest to safeguard humanity and our futures? Web3 may well be amenable to both prediction and deliberate design.

Though much of the web3 activity is centered around the financial industry, healthcare seems exquisitely suited to benefit from similar approaches. In fact, the potential gain in health value is expected to create a win-win-win outcome for citizens, healthcare, and retailers in the process. Indeed, with this tsunami of augmented intelligence, we have a responsibility to do more. We can better protect and uplift our human condition while launching the next inflection of wealth creation.

Unfortunately, nothing guarantees successful healthcare innovation, and even the efforts of the FAANG group and other big-name companies have fallen into disarray. For example, a JPMorgan, Berkshire Hathaway, and Amazon project, started in 2018, fell apart after a few short years.[12]

Meanwhile, without question, large retailers and healthcare players are using a widespread stream of our personal information in any number of unauthorized and unintended ways. Individuals are passive victims of large data mega-breeches, identity theft, and the steady monetization of our personal search secrets. At a time when workers question whether or not they should share their data with employers, our personal physical health expression continues to erode alarmingly. We are in a reckoning regarding data practices, AI, business models, and even our own biology.

Thankfully, society can address many of these issues by designing and delivering new, ubiquitous personal data practices. Healthcare transformation efforts have considered person-centric approaches for a long time. Today, using web3 tools, we can, in fact, augment current legacy approaches to ensure people prosper as we co-produce a more inclusive, participatory, and dynamic health intelligence—one capable of rewarding all contributors in perpetuity. We should settle for no less.

New thinking is needed—the type that restructures relationships between key stakeholders and generates widespread economic and health value across communities and businesses simultaneously. It's time for a new design that will get to the core of the problem, detaching the head of Buffett's tapeworm while propping up the healthy parts of the system: the medical miracles that keep us believing that American healthcare is the best.

WEB3 PROMISES CONTROL

Today, healthcare can account for a minority of outcomes using healthcare data alone. The majority of contributors to health exist outside of healthcare settings. Should health systems be consuming our data beyond our health visits? Given the rate of large data breaches and ransom attacks, this approach remains problematic. Must we remain merely visitors to our health data inside of industry coffers?

There is another way. George Gilder, in *Life after Google: The Fall of Big Data and the Rise of the Blockchain Economy*, reminds us of the centrality of knowledge in capitalism.[13] Without new knowledge, we cannot create real wealth. Human health expression is complex. This complexity exceeds current machine learning and depends instead upon humans teaching us which of them may be achieving various outcomes and why. What is reachable for any of us depends upon those who went before sharing the conditions and attributes of their creative human expression that collectively resulted in the best outcomes.

Likewise, uncovering the conditions that failed to deliver expected results leads to equally valuable insights. Today we cannot safely and privately search for others that share similar life trajectories. Imagine the knowledge our society could create if people could inform one another regarding conditions that were vital to achieve outlier experiences.

These are the early days in the transition to web3 frameworks, which make it possible for us to grant permission to our personal data for specific uses. Yet specific industries, such as the burgeoning cannabis industry, are taking advantage of web3 tools to deliver collective intelligence from communities to individuals—tools that both ensure regulatory compliance and secure sustainable business models.[14]

Can we achieve safe AI systems that reliably benefit from steady streams of human health creativity, while restoring data ownership and enabling private data exchanges? Early personal health data economies could provide such a path forward. Furthermore, through tokenization of personal data, as we'll discuss later, we can leverage personally controlled and permissioned digital assets to generate a plethora of new incentives as well as new products and services—ones that move the health industry from peddling average to delivering personalized reachability management to populations at scale, all while creating simultaneous wealth for industry and individuals.

Remarkably, the tailwinds for change are more surprising and aggressive than expected. COVID-19 has altered the physician-patient and worker-employer relationship. The crypto community is uncovering human behaviors in new ways, and naturally occurring remedies have been forced to forge a crowd-sourced path to confirming health benefits. These examples are putting new thinking in front of an ever-widening marketplace.

This is not to suggest that healthcare hasn't changed. After decades of considering remote care, COVID-19 forced many health systems into launching access to medical visits via the phone in the space of a few weeks. Though touted as transformative, this is really just converting a known analog model into a replica in the digital domain. A truly transformative and remarkably improved healthcare system will instead depend upon a participatory model that puts individuals at the center of their own health decisions—a truly patient-centric care model.

This design remains largely locked in presentation slide decks. It has yet to impact the technical or operational execution of healthcare. Thus, our preferred tech stack supporting patient-centric care does not yet fully exist. This stack would require new data management designs, participatory marketplaces, and authorized AI built on a foundation of collective cooperation.

THE RISE OF PERSONAL DATA ECONOMIES

Modern industries have taught us much about the value of personal data. These learnings, coupled with web3's distributed ledger technology (which we'll discuss later), provide fertile grounds for a new personal health data economy. This book helps map that journey for those in the medical *and* technology fields so we can knit together a group of diverse audiences with a common language to advance a shared vision for our preferred health future. We will discuss our on-the-ground reality—without being shy about the rough patches—focusing on where transformation is possible, where it is happening, and how these efforts pave a new way forward.

We begin the conversation by examining a number of truths that underscore the urgency in moving quickly. For example, population health expression is spiraling downward at an unprecedented rate, though the evidence of this remains largely hidden due to poor system design. Without dynamic and trusted evidence of harm, corrective action is dangerously delayed. Inaction will also widen our wealth gap and threaten the expansion of surplus populations—individuals who find themselves on the outside of society, who chronically lack the initiative, talent, wherewithal, or skills to contribute in meaningful ways.

When peering at the worst outcome imaginable, democracy and life as we know it hang in the balance if we fail to act. Democracy assumes that the majority experiencing good health will provide for the minority experiencing poor health. Would this assumption survive when the numbers flip? In the US, being overweight or obese is already much more common than having your ideal body weight.

Next, we will talk about the systems society must design to provide for widespread collaboration, working unitedly to deliver citizen-specific, personally relevant insights at a pace to match or even exceed the pace of tech advancement. Bound in the co-product of high-fidelity health intelligence, our new data partnerships will share wealth across the spectrum of contributors, including individual citizens, retailers, and traditional healthcare.

The COVID-19 tailwinds have already opened the door for citizen-led participatory scientific discovery; in short, people are more prepared than ever to manage data related to their health expression. Web3 actually provides for greater security while doing this. Using distributed ledger technology, zero-knowledge proof, and other tools, the power to protect individuals significantly exceeds that achieved to date. Even if motivations turn corrupt over time, built-in math can prevent bad actors.[15]

We'll discuss how, using web3 designs and principles, we can meet regulatory mandates, such as those outlined in the General Data Protection Regulation (GDPR) and the California Consumer Privacy Act (CCPA). We can also overcome the limitations of logic-based AI with parallel, free-living complex systems analysis. (If you don't understand all these terms right now, do not fear. Explanations will come.)

Other industries, including finance, retail, supply chain, and education, are ramping up new federated learning approaches as well as token-based incentive models. We're learning a lot. Healthcare—and you—will be in good company during this transformation.

I'll present a vision of what this future may look like and explain why it's essential for society. Whether we can arrive at this future together remains to be seen. I am not seeking a revolution, but I am asking that we do more than simply rearrange the chairs on the *Titanic*.

WHY FOCUS ON HEALTHCARE?

Having started off in math and physics, I was impressed with the ability of these disciplines to solve problems. With a few principles and equations, all manner of problem variations seemed to yield to computational explanations. Math and physics explained much of the spectrum of our real-world experiences, and efforts advanced, seemingly without constraint. Here the need for a clear path to a reliable business model was not present. Perhaps return on investment could surface in the future. Or then again, it might not.

Medicine is different. I assumed a medical education would set me up for purposeful work, but like many of my fellow students, I had a feeling of unease upon graduation. Is this it? Shouldn't there be more? We arrived thinking we would be able to problem-solve the entire spectrum of human conditions. Instead, the landscape of knowledge seemed remarkably patchy. Patchy in large part due to business-model and research-pattern constraints.

Imagine a three-dimensional landscape of medical knowledge with peaks of high understanding and valleys of little to no understanding. The valleys would far exceed the peaks in this horizon. On top of every peak would be dollar signs signifying business windfalls. We learn how to diagnose and manage lipid levels in our patients because the revenue opportunity is well established. Teams rush to rapidly standardize lab values across all labs because there is a drug that will lower this value, even though it is not a particularly good marker of heart disease.

Furthermore, patients often show up in the valleys. They don't quite fit the diagnostic criterion that would land them on a peak of knowledge. In order to offer evidence-based care, clinicians choose the closest peak, mentally moving the patient to a dollar-sign zone and providing the guideline-dictated care associated with that business model. Most likely, a prescription follows.

In math and physics, answers are mostly either correct or incorrect. In medicine, we're left with a range of possibilities and end up deciding to "try this" to see how well patients respond. This imprecision is even more unsettling when you consider our current, and highly impressive, technological capabilities.

We cut our teeth on business process optimization, and I was excited to see the flow of more math into medicine as we embraced big data, AI, and ML. Soon, a steady stream of scientific and personally relevant intelligence would surely fill the valleys of knowledge that plagued earlier approaches. Health intelligence would robustly span the spectrum of the human experience. Prevention could be a reality.

This has not happened.

The reasons are many. Some predate the internet; others involve technical constraints. There are design flaws, while data and power asymmetries persist.

A tidy mess has evolved on our watch. Patients bare their souls to physicians in the hopes of finding an answer, but over our careers, they really teach us daily about the gaps and valleys of knowledge in the health intelligence landscape. They deserve better. We can do better.

Clinicians see patients one by one, which is a laborious and slow path for driving systemic transformation. Thus, I moved into a chief medical officer position for one of the largest reference laboratories in the Pacific Northwest. We worked with a number of academic centers and startups, using technology to inform and shift health behaviors across populations.[16]

Though health outcomes improved, a surge in revenues was not apparent. Without impacting the bottom line, adoption proved difficult. Furthermore, generating new, robust, personally relevant health intelligence within current data practices was risky. Ensuring personal privacy and safety was challenging. The tech stack needed work.

After a decade in the C-suite, I began advising investors. Many barriers to success with health tech are not in the public domain. Investors and startups need access to industrial truths from those with on-the-ground experience. As more pitch decks included terms such as *distributed ledger technology*, *blockchain*, and *tokens*, I began to see that the need for investor education was obvious—especially for those who might avoid investing in solutions they don't fully understand.

Rather than choosing to self-learn in isolation, I began setting up investor education sessions. Eventually, one-off evening sessions advanced into a two-week boot camp on blockchain and crypto. It became clear: the possibility of robust privacy, security, and self-management of personal health data might in fact be within healthcare's grasp. A new tech stack was materializing—the arrival of web3.

HEALTHCARE OR SICKCARE?

The fundamental truth we must recognize and move beyond is that our current approach will continue to grossly underperform. In order to facilitate an optimally performing healthcare system, we must address and solve challenges related to personal identity management, trust, and health engagement, as well as ensuring economic windfalls are shared among even the smallest contributors. Is society ready? Whether or not we are, the use case for readying ourselves is in the process of writing itself.

Wealthcare advocates for a new design and seeks to simplify the complexities of moving from our current state to our preferred futures. Clay Shirky, in *Here Comes Everybody*, reminds us that humans are vaguely interested in actions that benefit us; however, if the option exists to benefit *the many*, *and* if the barrier to act is sufficiently low, we find it almost irresistible to act.[17] I hope to help lower the barriers of participation in designing a system that enables us to meaningfully contribute to our own economic and health benefits while also contributing to those of others.

Not every sector is ready to embrace what's coming, and healthcare may be the ultimate poster child for a sector that stalls in the face of advances. It doesn't have to be this way. As industries move to embrace more web3, healthcare can step ahead with a model that includes new data partnerships, greater transparency, improved security and advocacy, and the possibility of wealth creation that will dwarf the value of our current system.

Can we get there? Are the COVID-19 tailwinds enough to get us started in this new direction? Now is the time to roll up our sleeves and participate in reexamining our future and creating a health ecosystem that takes full advantage of web3's mathematically fortified internet. The net result will be a healthcare ecosystem that safeguards individuals and communities in new ways; provides new data-sharing and economic partnerships between individuals, providers, and retail giants; and ensures citizens enjoy widespread, purposeful living.

Ask yourself: Has today's internet shaped our society in non-altering ways? Are we locked into a healthcare reality where the farthest that innovation can go is to provide digital clones for existing analog processes?

To quote Yuval Harari, the future is not deterministic. In the face of new tools, new responsibilities arise. We have reached a health reinvention checkpoint, and the healthcare industry can forge a future that radically delivers the promise of universal access, intelligence at the pace of change, and mass customization to the individual-citizen level. Yes, *Wealthcare* targets an almost ideal system, one where the entire industry helps millions, perhaps billions, of people access optimal health expression. I'm willing to go there if it leads to an outcome that safeguards our information, expands personal wealth, and leads to smarter lives, rich with meaning and purpose, for all future generations.

We need each other more today than ever before if we are to

have any hope of accessing our full health and wealth potential. With many eyes, all bugs are shallow. Together we can get this done. Let's get started.

PRIMER: TOOLS FOR NEW THINKING

Throughout this book, you'll encounter key phrases that may require further explanation and discovery. For a comprehensive and up-to-date super glossary of terms, see "The Blockchain Super Glossary" by the Cascadia Blockchain Council.[18] This provides over 320 definitions that are updated regularly.

If you are already well versed in the web3 ethos, perhaps to the point of actively participating in one aspect or the other, feel free to skip ahead to Chapter I—or read on for a healthcare-centric way of viewing things.

MOVING FROM WEB1 TO WEB2 TO WEB3

Tim Berners Lee, known as TimBL, proposed and implemented an information management system in 1990 known as the World Wide Web (web1 for our purposes). As the *world wide* name implies, web1 was a distributed model—anyone with a connection could access information and communicate with each other.

This royalty-free technology was intended to be, and in practice was, easy to adopt. However, as the web advanced to support websites and online payments, it was clear that companies could leverage this technology to a much greater extent than individuals could. This resulted in an explosion of asymmetry. The once distributed web1 became the highly centralized web2, where massive companies continue to rule, thanks in part to business models built around advertising revenue. Over time, individuals traded in agency over their data for the convenience of "free" services.

About thirty years after the launch of web1, TimBL and others brought attention to these unintended consequences of web2 and proposed web3, a model that would re-decentralize the web, return agency to individuals, and make it easy to participate and personally own and manage digital assets within direct peer-to-peer transactions.

To be clear, web3 is only starting to make its way into our lives. Large companies still control the web, and it is still unclear to what extent we will achieve a decentralized internet. What is becoming clear is that web2 is sufficiently undesirable and bursting with marketplace misuse. This realization has many groups energized, if not passionate, about retooling and upgrading the web.

Once here on a mass scale, web3 is expected to launch the next era in wealth creation in the form of an ownership economy.[19] This will reduce reliance on intermediaries (banks, escrow, clearinghouses, etc.) and ensure collective value is redistributed to participants in perpetuity.

This sounds great, but does it have anything to do with healthcare? To start, healthcare as we know it came about long before the internet. Similarly to the web's evolution, healthcare has evolved to include a number of unintended consequences. Spend a week or two dealing with a medical issue, and we're brutally reminded of the many rough patches that make up our current healthcare system. There is no shortage of information asymmetry or marketplace misuse here.

Though healthcare has been touting transformation for decades, with web3, this industry may well enable an explosion of new wealth creation. Web3 has the power to support the individual as the workhorse of health knowledge creation, providing industry with access to *what matters most* to optimize health outcomes across populations.

UPGRADING IDENTITY MANAGEMENT: SSI

Identity matters. Privacy matters. However, some would have us assume that we don't really need privacy. Some say privacy only matters to those who have something to hide, and some tech giant CEOs have long suggested "privacy is dead; get over it."

Edward Snowden, in 2016, said it best: only needing privacy if you have something to hide is an antisocial argument. Privacy is the right to self, the right to a free mind. Privacy ensures that you can try out new ideas with your friends, family, and physician. Privacy may not be for the majority, who choose to fit into mainstream thinking and actions, but the minority, who might not fit in even in the smallest way, must have a right to privacy. Those who declare these groups are not different, and who intend to adapt to whatever the world expects, may be more willing to engage in *same*speak or *same*think. They might suggest that liberty or freedom is unnecessary.

Yet we should protect privacy for every generation. The physician-patient relationship is built on the right we all inherited to privacy, and as more and more private conversations move from in person to online, we have a responsibility to ensure that when analog goes digital, it carries the same or more protections. Thus, to start with, we need effective and personally controlled identity management.

Today, we all have hundreds of usernames and passwords. Every health portal dictates access requirements and has the power to revoke access at any time. We are mere visitors to our data, which large organizations house alongside the records of millions of other people. This is a data monarchy. These data storage warehouses—honeypots of data—suffer serious breaches and remain a prime target for ransom attacks.

The first step from data monarchies to data democracies supporting safe and secure self-management of personal health data includes the right to self-sovereign identity (SSI).[20] Don Tapscott, a giant in web3 discussions, states it well in *Harvard Business Review*:

> We need to address the real problem: that you don't own your virtual self. Each of us needs a self-sovereign and inalienable digital identity that is neither bestowed nor revocable by any central administrator and is enforceable in any context, in-person and online, anywhere in the world.[21]

Again, we're not there yet. Kaliya Young, one of the world's leading experts in SSI, and her team have been hosting the Internet Identity Workshop in order to provide guidelines for SSI, also called citizen-centric identity (CCI).

Our SSI would be a digital passport of sorts—a wallet that is locked to only one person. SSI cannot be revoked. Over time, it would be accepted across all health facilities and other businesses across the globe. No longer would our medical information end up mixed inside records for other people. Furthermore, our SSI could provide a means to truly own and manage our personal records in a seamless, easy-access way. As the custodian of our own data, we can decide to share, sell, or license it in ways that align with our values. This is the radical ethos of web3.

Still, it is unlikely that we will shrink our SSI down to a single version. Instead, we will most likely have a handful of versions that provide access to major networks, but this will be nothing like the hundreds of passwords littered across our current online activities. With unique and personal control of our identity, we will be better able to manage our health journeys. We will easily accumulate verifiable digital assets, such as clinic notes, lab values, device interrogations, images, and so on, onto our own longitudinal health records. This will set up a reshaping of power distribution and allow individuals participation in new markets. Together, both individuals and industry will benefit from web3 approaches expected to fuel the next inflection of wealth creation.

BLOCKCHAIN AND SMART CONTRACTS

We're not likely to get far into a web3 conversation without bringing up blockchains and smart contracts. Let's start with the legendary minds behind these relatively new tools.

Satoshi Nakamoto is a pseudonym for the person or persons who released a white paper in 2008 detailing a new way of managing digital cash transactions during the financial crisis in the US.[22] While Satoshi's true identity remains anonymous (therefore we'll use *they* as a pronoun), they not only produced a white paper, but also wrote the code to support the first use case: digital *cash*, well known today as the cryptocurrency Bitcoin (BTC), built on the bitcoin blockchain.

More than a decade later, Bitcoin not only remains in circulation, but as of this writing has peaked to over US$67,000 in November 2021 and dropped to hover around US$20,000. For more details, see the YouTube video *Legend of Satoshi Nakamoto* by Jill Carlson.

The word *cash* is key here. Some of us think that digital services, such as Venmo, PayPal, and others, serve the same purpose. However, in these examples, a few operators control the services that consult with banks, as well as various middle agents, in order to settle financial transactions. Typically, each intermediary scrapes off and pockets a percentage of the transaction.

However, when you and I are face-to-face, and I hand you twenty dollars cash, there is no bank or intermediary at all. The full sum goes in your pocket. Bitcoin is a close approximation of cash, but digital instead. It is both a direct peer-to-peer financial transaction solution and distributed at the same time: no central authority or leadership team per se manages the code base. Instead, the bitcoin blockchain depends on a wide number of participants ensuring that the system stays secure over time.

The bitcoin blockchain was purposely built to provide direct peer-to-peer transactions using Bitcoin. In other words, this blockchain provides property rights for eight billion people. It may be the strongest computer network that has or likely ever will exist.

Building on the success of the blockchain, it was clear that extending the peer-to-peer first use case to other more varied use cases would be valuable. To do this, it was necessary to build a new multipurpose blockchain.

In 2013, Vitalik Buterin, a young Russian-Canadian programmer, proposed and later built the ethereum network (a blockchain), which uses Ethereum (ETH) for transactions.[23] This second blockchain was designed with a more general-purpose scripting language that could support programmable transactions (smart contracts).[24]

This approach provided built-in auditability and immutability of blockchain, while supporting flexibility in defining the conditions under which various transactions would be executed. This technology lays the groundwork for data stream management to occur without bias and with full precision each and every time—an ideal property for personal health data management.

BLOCKCHAIN

Blockchain is a form of database. Unlike other databases, however, blockchain has specific and fairly rigid properties. It is an append-only data structure that exists in many distributed copies and requires consensus across a large number of entities to confirm validity of a new addition (or block) before it can be added to the chain. Collectively, these properties form the basis of what can be thought of as the mathematically fortified internet, or web3. Due to these special requirements, blockchains have some highly desirable attributes, as well as some that are less so.

There is built-in auditability, and the database is remarkably tamper-proof due to its consensus mechanism. Lack of a formal governing body suggests that humans are less likely to be able to derail the way the system was intended to work. However, if there's a problem, fixing it can be difficult when no one is in charge. Furthermore, blockchain protocols can be slow, expensive, and have environmentally challenging consensus mechanisms. Again, these are early days and there remains much work to be done.

CRYPTOCURRENCY

Cryptocurrency (crypto) is a form of digital money, also known as coin, that exists within payment systems that typically use encryption plus a distributed ledger, such as blockchain. The design largely ensures security of transactions between peers, such that banks, clearinghouses, currency exchanges, and other intermediaries may not be needed. Bitcoin was the first cryptocurrency, in 2009. Since then, more than eighteen thousand have emerged.[25] All coins since Bitcoin are by definition alternative (altcoins).

Crypto is the fuel of the value exchange grid, and many believe it represents the future of finance. In fact, Bitcoin is arguably the most robust form of money that mankind has ever invented. Its ideal monetary properties exceed gold, silver, fiat, and all currencies invented to date.[26]

Traditional government-issued money (the US dollar, for example) is a narrow expression of value. Using digitally native forms of currency, properties of these coins can be adjusted to serve specific functions. For instance, using banks and dollars for tiny loans or payments would be expensive. However, managing thousands of tiny loans or payments with crypto simply requires a few lines of code, a mere sequence of zeros and ones, and the intended transaction will happen flawlessly.

This property will be useful for health data marketplaces, where individuals could use and even receive crypto as payment for even the smallest micro-data contributions to algorithm-based products and services.

TOKENS

Tokens provide a means of tagging and tracking value that travels within and between various digital environments. By using tokens, value is not lost. In gaming, for instance, they are fundamental to defining a player's position among others within online games. Both Bitcoin and Ethereum are tokens, along with the thousands of altcoins that exist today. Many are considered security tokens, purchased with the intent to gain value, or a return on investment. Other tokens act like coupons: they provide access or discounts to services. Some can be exchanged for various rights or privileges, such as governance, proof, and ownership tokens. Tokens can provide *liquidity*, *staking*, and other benefits that are beyond our discussion here.

Can tokens help us learn how best to navigate our inevitable health mishaps? Will they be foundational in accumulating real-time understanding of personal and community challenges in time to make a difference? Can savvy token economics solve our health engagement challenges? The potential roles for tokens are many. This brings us to a special form of token, the NFT.

NFTS

An NFT (non-fungible token) is a specific type of token. To understand the nature of NFTs, let's start with the opposite, a fungible token. The US dollar is a perfect example. Every dollar is worth exactly the same as every other US dollar; therefore, we can trade dollars without any change in value. US dollars are fungible. If the value of the dollar goes up or down against any other currency, then the value of *all* US dollars goes up or down accordingly.

Non-fungible tokens are the exact opposite. No single NFT is the same as any other NFT. They cannot be traded. These digital certificates are unique, one-of-a-kind digital files that make it possible to digitally prove ownership of an asset. Because each song or each painting is unique, managing and transacting in artistic value helps to understand how NFTs can be useful. They cannot be copied and pasted, edited, deleted, or manipulated. Proof of ownership, authenticity, and provenance can all be locked into an NFT. In an ideal web3 scenario, NFTs will allow creators to track the use of their art and garner economic benefit with each and every use, according to programmable transactions or smart contracts that connect the artist directly to their audiences.

In a web3 health ecosystem, we can begin to convert our personal health expressions into digital assets and tag them with NFTs. Our personal health data alone may not be worth much, but when considered in aggregate with hundreds of others, new medically relevant truths will emerge. New knowledge is the backbone of new wealth, and NFTs will make it possible to track micro-contributions to new knowledge efficiently, effectively, and without missing anyone. This enables a future of robust health intelligence co-production, complete with nimble incentive models and royalty streams of passive income that may last into perpetuity.

The use of tokens in this way may very well take us from a participatory economy to an ownership economy and give us the tools we need to track our value creation along the way. Each of us will have a handful of wallets that manage a suite of tokens for various tracks and sub-tracks of our lives: health, education, vocation, real estate, legal, and so on. Increasingly, our tokens and wallets will be interchangeable as we navigate our physical and digital lives.

MINTING

Minting is a process that creates a pool of coins, tokens, or NFTs. This pool, typically millions or billions of tokens at a time, is defined with a number of attributes, which are authenticated on new blocks via a consensus mechanism. A fleet of geographically distributed computers work together to verify, validate, and time-stamp this new pool of tokens. Location, provenance of the information, and all subsequent transactions are verified and recorded using a blockchain-based ledger shared across distributed computers.

ZERO-KNOWLEDGE PROOF (ZKP)

ZKP is a token that results from an encryption software protocol that connects an individual prover with another person or verifier without revealing any private details. The ZKP token simply confirms whether something is true or not.

In healthcare, we may think of eligibility requirements for a certain procedure. A patient might submit a ZKP token to a clinic booking manager to verify that insurance will cover the payment. The booking manager does not need to be aware of any pending procedures or other personal information that might be part of a typical search through insurance-provider claims.

Another good example of ZKPs involves providing COVID-19 vaccine requirements. An individual can use a software solution to prove that they meet entrance requirements for a flight, a restaurant, an arena, and so on. People, or even scanners at the door, can scan their ZKP barcode and provide an "all good" green check mark to allow entrance. This result verifies that their vaccine status meets the requirements of admission without disclosing which combination of vaccines they received, or when and where.

ZKPs are an example of technology that lingered as an academic concept until the crypto community recognized the potential value of actually building the tool. Various stakeholders committed to pool resources, and in short order, US$25 million was available to deliver this important function. Early ZKP versions may be slow or expensive to utilize, but they provide another window into how a more private and secure future may realistically unfold.

DAO

A DAO (decentralized autonomous organization) takes advantage of all the previous information in order to set up a digitally native company—one without an office tower, lobby, boardroom, cubicles, or desks. Over time, even leadership oversight might go away. A *New York Magazine* article refers to DAOs as "blockchain-based co-ops with software constitutions."[27]

Typically with a DAO, a group of people settle on a common goal that requires communal efforts to achieve. They set up and lock in a treasury and operating plan (as code), which helps keep them on target rather than swaying in different directions. Then they go about raising and using funds according to their agreed-upon intent. Once the DAO is up and running, this originating group may no longer be necessary, as the software handles future decisions as directed and on an ongoing basis.

This model is attractive. For tech-savvy groups, the setup effort and time could be quite short. The lack of physical entities, buildings, and so on, means DAOs may have very little overhead. Plus, transparency is baked into the code—auditing should be relatively seamless. In short, DAOs can be a great way to lower the burden of getting stuff done.

They may teach us new and nimble ways to self-organize around online communities. Here, democratic values can thrive as members debate and vote on stakes, features, and products, and rely on contracts (encoded on the blockchain) to set and enforce regulations. Members calibrate and track each other's contribution via tokens—how much a person contributes by way of useful or insightful information, data, humor, and so on, comes back to them as tokenized rewards.

In healthcare, potential situations that might lend themselves to a DAO framework seem endless. Can a community that is hours away from the nearest MRI machine use a DAO to fix this problem? Tokens would track MRI funding contributions: dinners for donors, speeches, webinars, and so on. Smart contracts could issue tokens for discounts to individuals, should their family or friends need an MRI. There are many variations of this approach.

DAOs may be ideal for data unions as well (a pool of data gathered for specific purposes). The DAO will still need to raise money to pay individuals to share relevant bits of their health data. Likewise, the DAO may need to be able to accept money from purchasers of various combined sets of data.

DIGITAL FIDUCIARIES

Restoring individual agency in our digital lives will not be easy. We are likely to need help along the way. This help may come in the form of digital fiduciaries: professionals who set, periodically check, and update a suite of automatically executing software (smart contracts) on our behalf.

Let's briefly unpack this person-centric, data-driven future. First, there's a strong chance that a portion of society will not be interested in managing their own health data if and when the opportunity arrives. Others may be slightly interested but confused by the tech. Meanwhile, the data extraction behaviors of FAANG and others will continue as we proceed with online transactions. Digital fiduciaries can help protect us from unwanted extractions and thrive as professionals in an environment where individual users will turn to them for trusted management of their digital lives.

Most of us are already familiar with personal fiduciary agents, such as doctors and lawyers. Digital fiduciaries will help manage and check our preferences related to sharing and blocking data, working with certain providers, exercising base token rates required before opening access to data, and so on. Given what our online lives may look like in a web3 future, the role of the professional digital fiduciary may become an exciting professional track, especially for those who wish to niche-focus on specific areas of data-derived wealth management.

FEDERATED LEARNING

Today's biggest companies extract data to train prediction models (algorithms), which generate outsized profits. We, the users, have traded agency for convenience and are left without control or privacy over our online activities. But there is another way.

Federated learning is a machine learning process that provides companies with the ability to train prediction models. Rather than extracting and pooling our data into their own servers or data clouds, however, our data stays on our devices.

Here's a scenario: a company needs to predict the average

number of texts that people receive during work hours.[28] Using federated learning, a query or local model will arrive on our device and wait until our phone is idle. When the timing is right, the query will compute the number of texts per hour between 9 a.m. and 5 p.m. over a set number of workdays and then attach an average to an individualized string of digits. Neither our identities, nor the content of our texts, nor any other data will leave our phones. The digits alone will train the local model, and then this update will leave the phone. Repeat the same event on thousands of phones, and eventually all the local models train the central algorithm, which then has a strong ability to predict the number of texts throughout the workday.

In healthcare, we already use federated learning to build a better ability to detect which patients are likely to need more intensive care.[29] During COVID-19, for example, multiple hospitals collaborated to create a tool that would identify patients according to their likelihood of requiring supplemental oxygen. Now when you show up in the emergency room with your mother, who has a fever and a cough, she will benefit from the experiences of many patients who went before.

Hospitals hold on to patient data and permit training AI models to access specific items (e.g. chest X-rays, lab values, patient demographics) to boost the predictive power of the model. In this way, the AI only accesses very specific data, while the rest of our data remains private. The individual pieces of data do not move or pool. Instead, the model travels to the data, and harvests and pools improvements. This preserves patient privacy and generates a tool that will help predict whether your mother (in the above example) should be admitted in anticipation of needing supplemental oxygen.

Here's why this matters: when data leaves our personal interactions, with or mostly without our permission, we have no way of controlling any follow-on uses. Federated learning is privacy-first by design—a fact that means the process can deliver model training while returning our personal agency over our own data.

Having confidence their data will not leave their custody is likely to encourage people to willingly provide specific views into data, knowing that their personal information is safe. Add to this a rich overlay of tokens to incentivize participation, and layers of dramatic insights seem almost inevitable. This could lead to a type of web3 ownership economy that may well generate knowledge at a pace and scale we've only imagined.

THE METAVERSE

Our two-dimensional experience of screen calls and emails have conditioned us to clearly delineate between our in-person and online lives. A metaverse hopes to blur these lines. Instead of a 2D Zoom call, we (as one of our avatars) will meet colleagues in a 3D boardroom. Instead of having twenty tabs open on our screen, we don another piece of technology—typically glasses or headsets—with fitting acronyms: augmented, virtual, and mixed reality (AR, VR, and MR). This eliminates the need for tabs, while our screen takes on the 3D properties of virtual, simulated worlds that feel and *seem* like real life.

Moving to 3D provides advantages to businesses that rely on influencing consumers' behaviors by their surroundings. Recall the same reasons we have to fully walk to the back of the grocery store just to get a carton of milk. Thus, rather than checking off an online shopping list, a metaverse hopes that the three-dimensional farmers' market will ensure kiwis and kale make it into our shopping carts, even if they weren't on the list. Perhaps clothing that we might never have the confidence to wear in public will become in vogue in the metaverse as our avatars don *user skins* (digital-only clothing).

In healthcare, human anatomy is often inconveniently small. A good example is epidural anesthesia. Trainers are using VR glasses with students to help them navigate their virtual needles into epidural spaces that are ten or twenty times the actual size in real life. As the students' skills improve, the model size shrinks down to reality, and students can train on hundreds of attempts without harming anyone in the process. Eventually, surgeons in the metaverse may operate on our virtual bodies as a sort of dry run ahead of surgery.

If web3 is in its early days, the metaverse we may eventually know is even earlier. Still, the expectation is that these ideas will build on each other. A metaverse will assume an ownership economy. Our self-sovereign ID will make it easy to navigate between virtual rooms, buildings, landscapes, and countries. Most coins and tokens will be easy to use and often interchangeable. Setting up a DAO using an *off-the-shelf* code base may be a *thing* as companies set up operations within a metaverse instead of physical buildings.

Clearly we have much to learn. Remember that many things are simply not possible...until they are. There was a time when people thought they would never pay for anything online, but those days are over. We couldn't take a photo with a phone until we could. We couldn't make a call without a phone line until Voice over Internet Protocol (VoIP) allowed us to. We didn't have crypto until we did. A metaverse could shift the once impossible to the possible at a speed and scale we have yet to experience.

The medical literature is full of dramatic finds that rarely seem to translate into fully effective actions in real life: 69 percent less cancer, 91 percent less diabetes, 67 percent mortality reduction, and so on.[30] Will a 3D virtual work and play environment push compelling truths forward in ways that our 2D academic papers and online experiences struggled to achieve? The answer is likely a resounding no unless, that is, web3 and the metaverse succeed in reshaping our current data power distribution.

Facebook has rebranded to Meta Platforms, and other FAANG companies are marketing metaverse narratives. However, metaverse-speak for big tech may be more self-positioning than revolutionary. Where is the evidence that corporate-owned metaverses will adopt the ownership economy ethos of web3? Without changing the distribution of power, can a metaverse transition be revolutionary?

We have a chance to build tomorrow with new attitudes, tools, economic realities, and health outcomes. It will take changing the distribution of power to repair marketplace misuse and make the once impossible possible.

PART I

WHY WE NEED WEB3

CHAPTER ONE

OUR TECHNOLOGY PARADOX

Most of us have a working knowledge of healthcare basics. We're familiar with a number of key factors that drive poor health across the globe: poverty, low access to good nutrition, excess sedentary behavior, mental health traumas, exposure to toxins, and a myriad of other issues that create barriers to achieving optimal health. Less known, however, is that wealth and general prosperity provide very little protection against remarkably poor health in our modern world. Today, none of us can expect to be healthy by default.

Many people are convinced that suggesting individuals need to do a better job of maintaining their health is a hopeless endeavor. It is nearly impossible to motivate certain people to adopt healthy behaviors. Many have tried: we have graveyards full of wellness programs, employee point systems, treadmills, stationary bikes, and discarded fitness trackers. But success tends to land somewhere between fleeting and sporadic.

What follows is a case for a new approach. It starts with the fact that global health intelligence is grossly underperforming, traditional scientific approaches are inadequate, and we the people can no longer rely solely upon experts to decide when and how our health transactions should occur—screening, testing, examinations, and the like.

Fundamentally, we all suffer, regardless of socioeconomic status, ethnicity, education, or any number of factors, in a world where too little is known and even less is sufficiently and personally relevant to our needs. In this world, we cannot see around corners in time to make a difference.

The rails of web2 healthcare are too shallow for all of us, and we are derailing into unintended pathology at unacceptable rates. Modern societies should expect and achieve more. The fallout is huge.

This underscores our technological paradox: as tech improves, health declines.

As modern nations enjoy ever-impressive and enabling technology, populations suffer increasingly with widespread, preventable poor health. The widening gap between rising technology success and declining biological expression can be called a *reachability gap*: the growing distance between what citizens on the ground are experiencing and what we could *reach* if technology were expressly designed to safeguard and excel our biological expression. The inflection point—that point in time that arrests our biological decline and turns the ship around, thus providing society with a full-scale correction—likely coincides with the adoption of a web3 ownership economy ethos and all that it enables. Believe it or not, that time is here. Yet we continue to exist within unacceptably low levels of human-relevant intelligence. Why have we settled for less than optimal?

Old web2 industrial approaches, even those that take advantage of newly minted AI and machine learning, are insufficient to materially reverse this trend. The time for change is not only here, but it is also urgent.

This book proposes a data-rich future because, like it or not, we are not sliding away from more and more data. Yes, data can be dangerous, and society is slowly waking up to the perils of big businesses built on massive data extraction practices. Is this a contradiction to the prevailing winds? Are we further facilitating the problems we are seeking to solve? In short, no.

Max Tegmark, professor of physics at the Massachusetts Institute of Technology (MIT) and the president of the Future of Life Institute, reminds us that as humans, we have existed in our current form for about one hundred thousand years. If our futures include another hundred millennia, we will need to reinvent ourselves many times. Hopefully we can get it mostly right most of the time!

Our modern misuse of technology reminds us we don't know everything and that we need better processes in place if we wish to see around our blind corners. This recheck must result in our ability to dynamically respond to shifts in often unintended outcomes to avoid major mistakes.

For our youth, the need to act may be most urgent of all. They no longer have default access to their genetic potential. Teens can be seen routinely limiting, if not destroying, their future earnings potential through faulty physical and mental maturation. Through no fault of their own, these are disastrous outcomes that no one would knowingly sign up for if given the chance up front. Kids don't want this. Parents don't want this.

Determinants of future outcomes silently take shape years before they become evident. Once measurable, they are often largely irreversible. How cruel is it to rob a child of their full potential before they are old enough to know what is happening? Is it the added hormones in milk? Do extra pounds matter? Bottom line: due to our siloed approach to understanding health, we lack the insight to know for sure.

Preventable poor health has become a modern epidemic. It lasts decades yet remains quietly persistent as business models continue to prosper despite the greater ramifications. The healthcare industry as we know it continues to mostly run as *sickcare* at the expense of actually gaining a view into the ebb and flow of societal health expression.

ROUGH PATCHES AND DESIGN FLAWS

What follows are examples of specific rough patches and design flaws that affect our current healthcare and other industries, preventing us from reaching the reachable. You may be familiar with some, while others will surprise you. Most of these challenges have existed for decades, yet none have proven repairable within web2 technology. In listing these challenges, my goal is to present a compelling case that introduces the building blocks of web3 and sets the stage for a meaningful expansion of web3 solutions into the healthcare industry.

Technologically speaking, the things we can do today are truly astounding. What we'll do tomorrow, barring a catastrophe, will dwarf today's technological advances. To paraphrase Bill Gates, we tend to overestimate what will be possible in one year and grossly underestimate what will be possible in ten years.

Still, while we may live in exciting technological times, things are very much two-sided. On one hand, we can build and achieve more today than at any time in known history. On the other hand, cars, touch screens, smartphones, and nearly every other new advancement adds to a growing list of grossly unexpected and widespread human collateral damage. Since the early 2000s, social behavior has moved to web2, as we email, blog, vlog, text, tweet, and push content back and forth. While giving us new ways to connect and share, it has also proven problematic. We've only now begun waking up to a tremendous flood of unintended consequences and harms incurred through the massive and largely unauthorized capture and sale of our digital activities.

Shoshana Zuboff's *The Age of Surveillance Capitalism* details the evolution of modern business practices that generate multiple billion-dollar revenue models through ad optimization. One 2017 study found that even an improvement of 0.1 percent prediction accuracy would yield hundreds of millions of dollars in additional earnings.[31] Not only does this practice occur without explicit authorization from users, but the outsized wealth it creates does not find its way back to those same users who generate the data that drive ad-optimization insights.

This massive power imbalance of billions of dollars that *the few* enjoy at the expense of *the many* is a topic that Nick Vincent, a PhD candidate researching the dependence of modern computing technologies on human-generated data, and his colleagues at Northwestern University have covered. They describe a crime of data labor theft by the five most valuable tech companies in the US.[32] Of note, the five-company collective market cap was valued at $7 trillion in 2020. Vincent and others provide a short list of consumer actions that, if achieved at scale, might help shift corporate behaviors. We have a long way to go.

George Gilder's *Life after Google: The Fall of Big Data and the Rise of the Blockchain Economy* comes to mind as well. In the book, Gilder reminds us that, without doubt, internet security has reached crisis level.[33] Mega-breeches, identity theft, and ransom attacks are commonplace today. The core message is simple: security cannot be a technical afterthought, nor can it be solved within the current computer and network architecture. Without hardcore security built in at every transaction, every platform remains at risk. Going further, in his discussion of artificial intelligence, Gilder reminds us that by design, AI is based on logic—yet logic is not a universal theory, and reason alone does not explain everything.

One good example relates to AI-enabled drug discovery processes in place today. A human expert in complex systems described how AI was able to detect, based on the structure and charge of a specific drug candidate, whether the candidate would be able to enter the cell nucleus via the nuclear port (our biological doorway into the nucleus of our cells, where we store our DNA). Using this technology, hundreds of thousands of potential candidates could be screened for possible use in vaccine development. This approach has been met with varying success, but what shocked the audience was what the speaker said next:

> To be clear, holes remain in our understanding. Yellow fever vaccine was developed decades before our current AI approaches. Being curious, we took the yellow fever vaccine and submitted it to our software, the AI "kicked it out" suggesting according to the AI that this molecular structure would be useless as a vaccine candidate.

This is indeed what the AI came up with—essentially useless. In real life, our yellow fever vaccine remains one of the *most* effective vaccines ever developed. The fact that the AI gave it a failing grade is well worth our attention.

Clearly, AI understanding of three-dimensional structures and surface charge distribution remains insufficient to fully determine a candidate's ability to enter the nuclear port or generate a vaccine response. Perhaps our biology does not exist in two, three, or even twenty dimensions. Biological complexity continues to elude our full understanding and is likely to continue to elude logic-based algorithms. In this sense, as the ultimate purveyors of biological truths, we carry immense value that will not be easily replicated without our insights anytime soon. In other words, only people can define what is reachable *by* people at any time.

Beyond the argument of just how effective AI may or may not be in uncovering once hidden truths, we also must consider the threat of AI eclipsing human intelligence. Today, we seem to have landed on a widespread consensus that AI will indeed advance to harbor superior intelligence in specific areas in the very near future. Are humans writing our own destruction with advancing AI?

Max Tegmark, MIT physics professor, suggests in his book *Life 3.0: Being Human in the Age of Artificial Intelligence* that we need not assume superior intelligence always comes with the master-slave relationship so common in science fiction.[34] Another well-known intelligence hierarchy relationship is the simple parent-child relationship. In this model, intelligent parents are remarkably careful to provide safe guidance and protection of their children. Tegmark states that generating the parent-child relationship between AI and humans is not merely a technical design task. To this end, his team has set up the Future of Life Institute to deliver our much-needed design specifications, ensuring humankind survives and hopefully thrives over time.

While we're busy solving these looming technical challenges, we shouldn't lose sight of the fact that our biology actually has no knowledge any of this is happening. Our cells do not know that we carry a cell phone or that we are pumping out reams of code and generating mass automation all around us. No, our biological operating system continues to execute electrical and chemical transactions as it did hundreds of years ago. It still assumes a basic twenty-four-hour photoperiod, periodic nutrition in the form of farm foods, and a life full of activity to both gather nutrition and avoid encounters that may threaten our lives or long-term ability to survive.

Even though our cells and DNA may not be aware of the technical tsunami we're living through, our bodies are struggling to optimize within modern environmental conditions that massively outpace our capacity to adapt. The health system structures we've built within web2 are woefully inadequate for where we are and where we are going as a species. It is in need of a serious upgrade if we as biological units are to thrive.

To this end, perhaps we can see a more compelling example of our poorly performing health intelligence by examining the eroding health expression of younger cohorts. Today, more of our teenagers, unable to see around the corner, are becoming undereducated and undersocialized and are unknowingly eliminating large fractions of their future earnings within a few short years of puberty. This leads us back to that young man we named Troy.

CHAPTER TWO

SEX STEROIDS WITH NO BACKUP PLAN

Puberty is essentially a sex steroid event that occurs during a one-and-done period in our lives. We experience an onslaught of hormones that guide our bodies through a complex cascade from early teens to young adulthood, and all this might entail. We change physically, mentally, and emotionally without deliberately doing much of anything ourselves.

In the grand scheme of life, our puberty experience is rather short—less than half of a decade happens in a blink. Still, the experience is a complex pathway that leads to decades of adulthood rife with the purposeful futures we all desire. Every four years, an entire generation transitions through this very precarious set of biological options, and as with any one-shot deal, there's no do-over, second chance, or effective backup plan. This is a once-in-a-lifetime transformative opportunity that remains incompletely understood.

Troy, who we discussed in the Introduction, carried extra weight into his teens. Fat cells have been known to create and secrete hormones, including estrone, a female sex hormone, which can block or interfere with expected maturation processes. Now a young adult, he carries prominent breast tissue, an abdominal fat pad, and another fat pad above his pubis. He also has uncharacteristically small sex organs—almost as if puberty failed him.

Have modern times ushered our population into a world where puberty fails to occur as intended across large numbers of younger populations? Could it be that America is a poster child for this phenomenon? In the United States, nearly a third of adolescents are either overweight or obese.[35] Global studies reveal alterations in the timing and trends associated with puberty.[36] Are these teens missing out to various degrees on an optimal puberty? Are other modern nations (e.g. the UK, Canada, Australia, China) immune to these events? Sadly, data from the World Health Organization (WHO) suggest otherwise.[37]

TROY DID NOT ASK FOR THESE OUTCOMES

Though the detailed co-occurrences of Troy's experience might have been invisible, the resulting challenges remain much easier to see and measure over time. Troy takes antidepressants, mainly accepting samples because he rarely has the means to pay for prescriptions. His insurance, when he has some, is a patchwork of coverage that doesn't predictably cover all medical costs.

Entering the job market has not gone well. Troy hasn't held a steady job for longer than six months, and it's not from defiance or an inability to get along with others. In fact, there is nothing defiant or belligerent about this young man.

Troy is mild-mannered and polite. He has few strong opinions about things and doesn't seem to care that he only has a handful of friends. He doesn't cause problems, get into arguments, or take a stance on much. He would rather spend the day in front of a screen. Any game will do. He doesn't want to bother anyone and hopes that, this way, no one will bother him. He avoids anything that might prove difficult: the *big* exam, the *big* relationship, or the *big* job.

MISSING ONE'S GENETIC POTENTIAL

As a kid, Troy wasn't all that different from other members of his cohort. At birth, it looked as if he had won the genetic lottery. Based on his pedigree, circumstances, race, ethnicity, and his family's education and socioeconomic status, the path to a successful life seemed to be laid out in front of him. Both his parents were successful in their fields—medical and legal. Despite being busy and working in demanding careers, they regularly helped their child with school assignments, introduced him to a number of sports and outdoor activities when he was young, and encouraged him to try new things, to seek his own answers, and to get right back up whenever he fell. He was loved but not coddled; scrapes and bruises were okay in his house, as were dirty hands and grass-stained jeans.

In school, Troy's earliest report cards were average—first a steady row of S's for "satisfactory," then B's once traditional grading kicked in. Soon, as the academic climb became steeper, Troy's grades began to level out at a low-B average, eventually settling into the C territory as he moved through middle school. He was smart, his teachers shared again and again, but seemed disinterested and lacked an innate motivation to push for more. Maybe he was bored, his parents wondered, or needed more challenges. No one was quite sure.

His parents found themselves asking other parents about healthy snacks and nutrition, reconsidering the school lunch menu, and once again talking with Troy's doctors. They quickly reached the limits of their research and fell into a default pattern that suggested things would eventually right themselves on their own.

As he approached his late teens, Troy's entry into the adult world did not go smoothly. Job applications yielded no tangible work, and hiring managers were hard-pressed to see much potential for even the most basic position, regardless of the industry.

How did this happen? Troy's issues were likely not related to poverty, ethnicity, race, privilege, or opportunities. At birth and throughout the early days of his life, the cards were stacked in his favor. No doubt, Troy's troubles did not begin overnight. As with many people in his cohort, they were the accumulation of hundreds of co-occurrences throughout the early decades of life.

Options were wide, given his circumstances—as were the chances to get things *slightly wrong* day after day, over and over again. Troy, like many toddlers, was a picky eater. He loved cold cereals and crackers, and little else. Fish and vegetables rarely, if ever, graced his plate. Before he hit middle school, fast foods became his meal of choice, and his parents had the financial means to support his preferences. By the time he was ten years old, he was already carrying extra weight. While fat cells (adipo-

cytes) may seem benign, as mentioned, they can generate sex
steroids, which, in an excess amount, may alter the complex
cascades of puberty.

How much sugar or screen time was too much? How were his
parents to know for sure? In Troy's case, were extra calories
the first contributors to knock his puberty off course? Did
hormone-laden milk play a role? Are other toxins to blame?
Who's to know? Despite being introduced to many sports, Troy
lacked confidence and quickly lost interest. Books and screen
time became pleasant escapes—they never made him feel *bad*
about himself. Soon gaming captured his mind, and he spent
many more hours on his devices than he did running, jumping,
or anticipating another player coming his way.

How could things as mundane as childhood meal choices or
choosing screen time over sports dictate so much in a person's
adult life? The fact is, the story of Troy is not unique. Nearly 33
percent of his cohort find themselves in similar situations in
their young adult life. Is there something unique about today's
youth that makes them more susceptible to these types of lifestyle adaptations? Why were past generations spared?

THE ACCIDENTAL WELLNESS OF PREVIOUS GENERATIONS

Did puberty progress with accidental correctness for previous
generations? Were teens spared any hope of messing up their
intended hormonal messaging during these sensitive years? We
know our collective genetic material has not changed between
generations; what we do with our genes, namely our genetic
expression, has changed in ways that we do not fully understand.

New genetic material is the result of centuries of biological evolution in response to shifting environmental influences, which can take many centuries to accomplish. In fact, the evolutionary drive from apes to bipedal *Homo sapiens* took roughly two hundred thousand years. Thus, gene disposition (the genes we are born with, i.e. the cards we were dealt) are not to blame. Given the same genetic starter pack, each new generation *should* expect to be at least as smart, as strong, and as driven to succeed as the previous. However, gene expression—the way we play our cards—is what *has* changed dramatically in the last few decades.

It's easy to track a series of events that led us here: we invented trans-fatty acids; moved away from traditional farming practices toward factory foods; invented school drop-off lines rather than having our kids walk or bike to school; started driving children everywhere to keep them safe; and started handing them our phones and tablets, then their own phones and tablets, to entertain, educate, and keep them quiet. We created a society where screens have become ubiquitous to the point where gaming is now a professional track.

Troy's parents played his hand for him at a time when he was too young to be responsible for making his own choices. They did their best to explore what was happening, but the tools that could have given them a deeper understanding of the possible ramifications did not exist in web1 and still do not exist in web2. How could they have known or gained a sense that what they were doing by way of food choices, activity, and screen time would somehow negatively and irreversibly impact their son's future?

Troy's parents are a microcosm of a much larger society that is perpetuating this reality without understanding the repercussions. We as a society aren't making the connection between the adults we are creating and what this means for population health and wealth over time.

One of the main differences between Troy's cohort and those of his parents and grandparents is that the latter are among the last of what we'll call *accidentally well.* Three decades earlier, Troy's parents were raised by mothers that did not have to know how to feed, exercise, or socialize their children to ensure that they would enjoy high-performing lifestyles during adulthood. During their youth, society ran with defaults that safeguarded them in ways that ensured most had good access to their genetic potential.

Perhaps this was a time of blissful biological laziness without significant repercussions. By and large, the food people ate was closer to the source and quite often was farm-fresh. Troy's parents, born at the tail end of the baby boom, grew up eating mostly whole foods and only began to shift their diets toward factory or fast foods in their midthirties, long after the sex steroid period of puberty. Life involved ample walking, running, and the types of chores that might come across as *child labor* in today's hypersensitive world. Having a TV was a luxury that no one took for granted, and common household chores kept them moving in and around the house.

To be fair, living conditions like these still exist today in many parts of the world. However, as we narrow our view to Western developed nations, we see that Troy is not an outlier. In 2020, the WHO reported that 80 percent of youth are not active enough.[38] Poor activity and eating habits are associated with negative long-term health outcomes, unemployment, and lower social well-being.[39] The fact is, large portions of Troy's generation—and all generations that follow—will no longer be accidentally well, which in turn dictates that they will not have *accidental access* to their full genetic potential. Instead, they will need to deliberately colocate the conditions that matter most, a task that will require a crowd-based approach to gathering and disseminating up-to-date intelligence.

We carry on with our busy lives, not paying attention to the fact that our biological operating systems still assume conditions that were present hundreds of years ago but are no longer present today. Troy's genetic disposition at birth was strong, but a myriad of environmental influences, choices, and decisions— some his, some belonging to his parents—conspired to dictate his current health expression: Type II diabetes, early fatty liver disease, lack of steady employment, and a nearly absent social network. Sadly, neither Troy nor his parents provided any level of *informed consent* for these outcomes.

HEALTH OUTCOMES FOR FEMALES

Girls are not immune to the silent perils of modern living either. Early onset puberty at six or seven years of age has been reported.[40] The two brief stories that follow, both about young women, serve multiple purposes. The first, about Hadeel, discusses how diet and physical activity impact fertility; it is also an example of how, through aggregating data, we can track co-occurrences and hopefully turn the tide toward optimal. The second, about Trisha, discusses disease and delves into the difficulties of continuing to navigate modern life without having full access to seeing around corners.

HADEEL

Hadeel is a young newlywed in the United Arab Emirates (UAE). As is common to this part of the globe, couples are expected to become pregnant within a year of marriage. Should the new bride fail to conceive over the first twelve months, it becomes likely that her parents and in-laws will see fit to intervene. At this point, all manner of fertility heroics may find their way into the situation.

Like much of life, successful ovulation and fertilization are the result of many complex moving parts. Increasingly, a link between lifestyle-generated insulin resistance and suboptimal ovulation has found its way into the conversation.

For many women in the UAE, being able to openly exercise can be difficult. Meanwhile, the abundance of refined carbohydrate options for snacking has exploded in recent years. If Hadeel were to optimize her diet and activity level, would this impact her fertility? Could she and other women in her situation avoid hormonal extremes of assisted fertility via medical interventions?

Today there's mounting interest in answering questions like these. Startups are providing apps to help women track menstrual cycles, along with other relevant co-occurrences. Together, they are uncovering ways to ensure that optimal baseline ovulation occurs, specific to them and their location.

Thankfully, pregnancy provides a fabulous and clearly measured outcome that takes only months to achieve. This new data stream of co-occurrences will eventually be able to train new AI and provide a steady corrective capacity to reset algorithms as conditions change on the ground. Imagine a future of widespread overt exercise becoming the norm for all genders in the UAE!

TRISHA

Roughly two hundred thousand women are diagnosed with breast cancer every year in the US. Trisha was diagnosed with breast cancer at a relatively early age—her early thirties. Was it heredity? Had she been predisposed since before birth? While a woman can inherit a genetic mutation, such as BRCAI or BRCA2, from a parent, heredity accounts for a mere 5 to 10 percent of such cases.[41] What co-occurrences account for the other 90 percent? What roles do weight gain, activity levels, or nutrition play?

For her part, Trisha had been an active teen and still maintains a fairly healthy lifestyle—weekly trips to the gym, casual biking and hiking, yoga, and so on. While she doesn't have the world's greatest diet, it's well-rounded and has always included plenty of vegetables and lean proteins. In fact, she was a vegetarian through high school and college, and only eats meat once or twice a week.

Again, traditional healthcare's guardrails, and our web2 reality, remain too shallow for us to dive into critical details in a high-fidelity manner, much less put them to work for us in real time. The same is true on the other side of the equation: hundreds of thousands of women derail from the path of optimal health every year, yet for unknown reasons, many will not develop cancer. Why are these women *not* diagnosed with cancer, whereas someone like Trisha was? Why don't we know these answers by now?

Hundreds of thousands of women have evaded a breast cancer diagnosis. If it were possible, in nonintrusive ways, to digitize their health behaviors (think intermittent use of wearable technology to track movement, nutrition, sleep, and so on)...and if women could securely share their experiences without compromising their identity...and if tokenized incentives drove a swarm of sharing behaviors...it would be possible to query these details and frame a highly personal, relevant path to optimize the avoidance of cancer.

These are a lot of *ifs*. However, web3 approaches help to make each one a reality as if each domino were falling on top of the next one.

Surely, if any of this were possible, wouldn't it have happened already? Let's glance at the design flaws of web2 health to better understand the inertia that plagues this industry.

CHAPTER THREE

WHAT CAN WE EXPECT FROM *SICKCARE?*

As mentioned already, healthcare cannot manage the myriad of co-occurrences that dictate future outcomes widely available to all of us. The industry as we know it is not equipped to grant us the chance to see around corners in time to make a difference.

Since their inception, traditional medical schools have provided healthcare experts with a strong starter package of knowledge. Then, with years of patient care, everyone that visits the clinic or hospital carries in with them new experiences and information that help craft a deeper understanding of our human condition.

Additionally, with career changes from frontline medicine to medical administration to clinical research, some professionals amass a diverse experience and have a clearer view into how pieces fit together, where blind spots exist, and what the health and wealth implications of those missing pieces are. These professionals may go far to inform our understanding of the current state of affairs.

However, most clinicians spend the majority of their careers inside a narrow stream of healthcare delivery. They don't practice outside of their lanes. Yet each patient exists within systems that span *all* lanes: neuro, ortho, gastro, and on and on. This level of individual complexity makes it impossible to fully consider all contributors or co-occurrences associated with any particular complaint.

In short, there are too many moving parts for our human brains to manage. We can't expect health practitioners to understand our detailed complexities while their exposure to us exists only as discrete moments in time, looking at small packages or single lanes of our lives.

As technology marches on, options expand almost infinitely. Thus, the option to *get living wrong* also expands. Luckily, our biology can and does manage to absorb our stream of mistakes, but only up to a point.

We can make small mistakes for months, years, and sometimes decades before our biology lets us know that we've hit a time-out: our college-aged smoking habit leads to a chronic cough and susceptibility to bronchial issues in our late twenties; our pancreas tips into Type II diabetes; our liver has become overwhelmingly laden with fat. In short, we are well until we are diagnosed as ill, despite the fact that we had been making our way *toward* ill for months, years, and sometimes, decades.

Most preventable poor health is the result of chronic malaligned behaviors, a myriad of moving parts that don't lend themselves to traditional methods of research. Massive numbers of complex co-occurrences that drive ultimate outcomes are beyond the AI and ML that can be applied to encounter data alone. We need more comprehensive data training our AI models, plus a steady stream of on-the-ground experience: a continuous *ground truth* to work in parallel. Together, AI models plus a robust ground truth will deliver a reliable understanding of what is around the corner for a specific individual in time to make a difference.

MANAGING THE MUNDANE

Our traditional medical model was built on the assumption that all people are well until they're diagnosed as being ill. For decades, the translation was simple: we could freely exist in our communities, and as long as we could rely on things like clean air, potable water, wholesome food, and daily physical activity, we would, by default, reach our full genetic potential. There's a sad bit of irony here: while outgoing generations—Troy's grandparents' generation, for instance—blissfully enjoyed accidental wellness, the world was moving in ways that would eventually hinder the ability for future generations to do the same.

If we were to measure and grade how well older generations designed and implemented a system to create and sustain optimal prosperity for the masses, we'd have to give them *fails* across the board. Just think about it: for centuries, the chronic diseases of aging occurred, by definition, in the aged. Now many chronic diseases occur prematurely, not by weeks or months, but by decades. For example, Troy's Type II diabetes, once called "adult-onset diabetes," increasingly accounts for more than 53 percent of pediatric diabetes.[42]

Let me make clear that the point is not to beat up on healthcare. Medical miracles happen all of the time. Trauma victims receive rapid diagnosis; medicines shuttle across the globe at record paces; a headache becomes a hemorrhage, but thanks to specialists and rapid responders, the result is a survivor's story with a positive ending. Healthcare excels when responding to urgent, critical needs—but not so well when dealing with illness or death by thousands of micro-events.

MISALIGNED INCENTIVES

Any discussion of healthcare's rough patches would be inadequate if we failed to mention the abundance of misaligned incentives. Many agree that any fee-for-service model incentivizes more services and not more health. We see disincentives in the form of modest penalties if patients are readmitted too soon after discharge. However, disincentives are rare for many other healthcare missteps. Take misdiagnoses, for example. These may not only go unpenalized but also untracked, as patients exit from one service to another to another. The next hospital system does not share data with the previous hospital, which labels them as having "failed to follow up." Without access to error, course correction is at least stalled, if not impossible. Patients suffer without the ability to protect future patients from similar mishaps.

Less-known misaligned incentives include the fact that doctors can sometimes make more money by prescribing more expensive medications. Andrew Toy, CEO of Clover Health, reminds us that some oncologists who infuse chemo drugs receive a percentage of the drug cost, in some cases up to 6 percent, as part of their fee.[43] That means that doctors may have disincentives to prescribe generics or lower-cost treatments—they will get paid more to prescribe more expensive infusion-dependant therapies. Rebates (discussed later) are another obscure form of pseudo kickback.

HEALTH APPS DO NOT EQUAL INNOVATION

Web2 technology keeps patients distributed across multiple systems, with little ability to connect the dots. This ensures suboptimal financial practices are relatively free to continue without public pushback. The system is simply too complex to connect the dots in any meaningful way. Can tech and social justice combine to deliver innovation?

When you explore healthcare from a broad view, you do see teams dedicated to innovation. They seek to provide new digital approaches to the daily workflow of analog medical processes. Rather than use in-house medical staff, many systems hire brand and customer behavior experts to help the industry stand up digital products and services or apps so patients can better navigate the *current* model.

Unfortunately, this incremental form of innovation isn't doing much more than converting analog processes to the convenience of mobile digital solutions. The instructions and user flow may change, but the core service model remains the same. The power structure and data governance models are unaffected. They may be lessening the mental burden that people face by trying to navigate their local healthcare system, but they are failing to provide meaningful upgrades to the existing data paradigm.

The same might be said for the retail side, where FAANG-level businesses hire seasoned health professionals who train them on the *current* model. Both approaches are typically constrained by web2 data models which, as mentioned, have been under-delivering health intelligence for decades.

There remains a plethora of untapped new products and services that could be unleashed by whichever stakeholders beat the path to citizen-centric data structures. Will healthcare or retailers capitalize on the opportunity first?

WITH WEB3, AN OWNERSHIP ECONOMY CAN DELIVER NEW RAILS

What if we were to suggest audacious goals and lay a framework for true health and wealth innovation? What would it look like? While we are awash with health fallout across our communities, tech enjoys unbridled innovation. Outside of healthcare, the financial sector is nervously learning about new web3 solutions such as Bitcoin, Etherum, and the endless host of altcoins that continue to follow—setting off a cascade of digitally native solutions for managing value. Enthusiasts are keen to shift from our highly centralized web2 structures to mostly decentralized replacements where possible. In the meantime, private blockchains offer a smoother on-ramp for early entrants.

Businesses are using blockchain and smart contracts to better streamline repeatable processes, the mundane events that slow operations and negatively impact their bottom line. They use business management systems to constantly update targets and further refine what is reachable. In doing so, these businesses outpace the old competition and uncover expanding existing, as well as new, markets. These processes could be imported into the way we do health, and doing so would go a long way to solving the web2 rough patches that have eluded correction until now.

What steps would healthcare take to move beyond *normal* and begin providing personally relevant *optimal* health targets to individuals? What shape would this transformation take? At the bare minimum, the components are likely to include the following:

- We as individuals would possess our entire longitudinal health, life, and wealth record, which acts as our digital homebase and follows us throughout the decades of our lives.
- These longitudinal personal data streams would become both a health and economic asset for each individual and their community.
- We would use our homebase to transact on demand with providers anywhere on the globe, regardless of where we work, play, or travel.
- We would co-create a massive lift in dynamic and relevant health intelligence and value as a collective, with the individual citizen as both the workhorse and co-benefactor of new wealth creation.
- We would use web3 to provide easy and reliable ways to pre-authorize the use of our data inside marketplaces, research, and other projects with which we share common goals.
- We would be assured of a complete and automatic audit trail that tells us which parties have accessed our data at what time, and for which purposes.
- In step with our leap in health-related intelligence, we would generate a massive increase in personally relevant and targeted healthcare messaging. Hopefully this is accompanied

by a meaningful elimination of blanket irrelevant recommendations or mass-marketing suggestions.

- We would replace *normal* with *optimal*, as defined by the crowd, and begin a future of real-world "reachability" management instead of peddling mediocrity.
- We would create and attach NFTs to personal health expression in order to incentivize sustained adoption, manage transactions, and quantify collaborative value generated.

Though genes take many millennia to adjust, technology can deliver new devices and software upgrades over the weekend. Just think of how often you receive an alert on your phone about an upgrade to your operating system. In no way can human biology keep up with the pace of change we see and experience on a daily basis—and the costs associated with this evolutionary slowness are huge.

Troy and Hadeel's generation may be among the first to lose out on being *accidentally well*, but they will not be the last. In fact, short of a global cataclysm that turns us all into hunter-gatherers again, no future generation in the modern world will ever be accidentally well again.

Following this arc, we require access to crowd-based relevant micro-event streams. With this access, informed consent to our futures becomes possible. We can choose prudent adjustments and optimize our health trajectories or suffer preventable underperformance in most domains of human functioning.

To do nothing might be the worst-case scenario. Unbridled mundane micro-event streams silently threaten to generate the world's largest ever group of what health experts and futurists alike call *surplus individuals*—people much like Troy, for whom the prospects of achieving a self-sufficient future are low.[44] Forget the high-functioning, purposeful career that his parents had imagined for him.

This phenomenon is not simply a local, regional, or even national issue. As much as it's worth wondering what this means for the future of American competitiveness, there's a much bigger question at play: What does this mean for the survival of the human race?

Maturing a web3 ecosystem will involve solving a number of challenges: What does this look like? How do we get started? Where is the money? How do healthcare, FAANG, and the government contribute and benefit? Part II of this book provides early answers to these questions in the hope that the broader stakeholder group will be inspired and enabled with a collective vision. Unfortunately, it's no simple task.

MAKING THE ONCE UNKNOWABLE KNOWN

In short, we have no business knowing as little as we know today. With great technology comes great responsibility. Troy's health journey might have been avoided if his generation *did health* differently. Knowing now that all future generations will no longer be accidentally well, we'll need to redesign the way we all do health. We can't do it alone. We need each other. Together we can safely and securely generate a dynamic collective intelligence that would underpin our ability to deliberately design our own health futures and reliably provide each generation access to the keys of their own genetic potential.

Can this be done? Will doing so improve the bottom line for

industry? No margin, no mission. Who will do it? Are the retailers (e.g. Walmart, Amazon, Google) already too far along for traditional healthcare to catch up?

Alex Mashinsky, CEO of Celsius Network, argues that it's impossible to fix the levels of greed that exist within our current financial system and that we shouldn't even try.[45] Instead, it would be easier to create a new parallel model and allow those who wish to opt in to do just that.

If web2 structures remain impotent to transformation, then web3 may just be the blue pill needed to set society on a much-improved course. We need not be charged with turning the *Titanic*; instead, our reset option would include building new personal health technology that acts as new rails, creating new opportunities and solving our collective challenges while preparing for new ones lurking around the corner beyond our current scope of vision.

Yes, healthcare is imperfect, but for plenty of people—individuals, providers, and large corporations—it is *close enough*. Mass change may simply not be in their future vision, which is fine. But for those who want more and who believe that more is within our reach, a new model may indeed already be forming within the expanding universe of web3.

Once we accept that society is no longer accidentally well, we can also agree that future generations *must* have tools in place to ensure that they *can* deliberately accumulate the oft-mundane co-occurrences that ensure access to their full genetic potential. This begins with a new attitude to how we *do* health as a society. What are our responsibilities to ourselves and each other? Let's keep the healthcare ecosystem parts that create the miracles while recognizing that we need to adopt an entirely new parallel approach—very much a *by the people, for the people* living-by-design approach.

The future is indeed a moving target, and we each find ourselves at different points in the journey toward a preferred tomorrow. An African proverb suggests that if we want to go fast, go alone; if we want to go far, go together. A central thesis of this book, especially as we turn toward Part II, is that health is more than a team sport—it's a global endeavor. Diversity carries immense value. The more we can access each other's health expression, the greater our ability to make sense of our own.

PART II

OF THE MANY

CHAPTER FOUR

CROWDSOURCING IS POISED FOR AN UPGRADE

Health is the result of hundreds of moving parts. Given the complexities of our time, we are in a state of greater person-to-person and group-to-group interdependencies than ever before. To date, we have only begun to harness the power of the collective to inform the individual, and vice versa: to share our personal insights into a matrix that enhances the collective knowledge. Some examples from everyday life include:

- PatientsLikeMe, an online community offering peer support, personalized health insights, tailored digital health services, and patient-friendly clinical education
- Crohn's and colitis communities
- American Arthritis Society, Alzheimer's Association
- 23andMe, Ancestry.com
- Various online social groups

Though we can and do generate crowdsourced intelligence, individuals remain locked out of the governance and control of these web2 approaches. Platforms such as those above group individuals by disease type and offer a place to share life experiences. The hope is to gather the experiences of the many in order to help inform everyone and keep future patients from having to reinvent the wheel.

These groups wax and wane in terms of committed participation and the value they produce. Few platforms, if any, provide a participatory model of governance, meaningful group decision-making, or reliable value distribution. Instead, leadership controls any value the collective creates and may not even report to contributors in tangible ways.

Still, despite their inadequacies, these models are a great first step in giving voice to the free-living system: groups of people with unique daily challenges specific to their life situations. These models provide details that exceed the scope of traditional scientific efforts but routinely and inevitably plague real-life encounters. However, because these efforts are not connected and form many siloed patient communities, the result is a resounding *digital silence* regarding the overarching and interdependent phenomenon that may be driving the bulk of human collateral damage. In other words, even as data continue to compile, these systems do not allow participants to see *into* or query: to infer, or make use of, what might otherwise be knowable.

EVIDENCE-BASED MEDICINE VERSUS EXPERIENCE-BASED HEALTH

Medicine has a long history of seeking to provide a clear evidence base for any given care pathway. Though ideal in theory, there are many gaps in practice. Randomized controlled trials, the workhorse of evidence-based practices, seek to stop all variables from moving while only the element in question varies. Answering a question such as "Does supplemental vitamin E impact cardiac health?" is extremely difficult. We are not able to control for all the confounding factors that exist within widely diverse populations.

How does vitamin E from nutritional sources differ from supplemental or a capsule form of vitamin E? Does Mother Nature supply enabling agents that make a difference in the ultimate function of vitamin E? If we are less aware of the functional details within the packages nature supplies, we're unlikely to generate a similar benefit from a capsulated form of vitamin E. Even if we were able to find a way to control a multitude of variables within a study population, how would these outcomes translate beyond those within the study?

Personal health expression should and could be informed by the experience of many. However, we need a better design to ensure that sharing our health information is both safe and effective and that it occurs on our own terms. This is a tall order. Without interrupting our massive medical machine, it is possible to set up new collaborative experiments. These could be designed to teach us, in real time, the incentive models that promote the best outcomes across diverse populations.

A web3 ownership economy model could yield a dramatic paradigm shift. As the locus of control of our data, citizens would be able to contribute to multiple collective data commons or trust engines—and would be able to do so in real time. This would help create a secure path to uncovering experience-based answers to personally relevant queries. Furthermore, citizens in a web3 model could benefit financially for individual contributions to collective value created if governance models were designed to do so—a topic we'll explore in greater detail in Part III.

Today, most industry giants are built on tech (and business models) that do not directly support this possibility. They seek to make populations readable for corporate gain. We should *expect* that digital services and apps cannot exploit us, yet we *accept* the opposite. Why? And how can we shift our expectation toward the idea that society must move forward together, based on shared principles and values over time? To do so, we need a new experience-based health model—one that supports a crowdsourced economy that builds and sustains a future that celebrates our interdependencies while creating personal intelligence and wealth at the pace of change.

DATA AND THE DEMANDS OF THE MANY

Another wrinkle that currently blocks optimal personal health intelligence is the fact that health systems continue to treat us as mass populations, not as individuals. Data, in the form of population health expression, feed the algorithms that make recommendations.

Take health screening practices, for instance. People receive screenings in the hopes of preventing the onset of premature adverse health outcomes; however, these screenings are often little more than case-finding efforts.

Preventive screenings for diabetes and lipid disorders depend upon there being a *sufficient prevalence of the disease* in a given population before an individual screening can be justified. It's like living in a neighborhood where certain four-way intersections lack stop signs in all directions; when you seek the addition of a stop sign, city officials explain that there haven't been enough accidents in that location to warrant the cost. Once things *get bad enough*, then the city will worry about installing a sign or two.

When screening means little more than case-finding, it ensures that medical professionals can introduce medication or other therapies in time to avoid further deterioration. Ideally, ongoing personalized preventative screening would identify the data streams of an individual's health journey in time to fully avoid arriving at the point of even needing care.

Our dichotomous approach to evaluating health as being *normal* or *abnormal* may be an artifact of using trained humans to deliver the bulk of medical services. Despite our egos, degrees, plaques, and all manner of accomplishments, human brains are remarkably limited. We do not possess the innate computing power to manage hundreds of moving considerations simultaneously. Thus, human experts are equipped to consider remarkably few variables when determining, for instance, if a prescription is warranted or not.

While medicine holds on to practices that trained individuals can deliver, other industries have yielded to and accepted business intelligence and complex computing. Machines capable of managing large volumes of co-occurrence data continuously analyze insights to pull out interdependencies that drive desired outcomes. Healthcare, on the other hand, might utilize a considerable amount of business intelligence or complex computing for revenue cycle and workflow optimization, but not for capturing information about an individual to provide personally relevant laboratory thresholds. Could crowdsourced ways ensure that targets are specific for personally chosen health trajectories?

If society wishes to transform and improve the health of the many, we'll need to deliberately process data that represents the multiple alternative health tracks of diverse populations. This is the path for helping communities transition from living blindly to deliberately co-designing their own health futures.

For years, healthcare has succeeded in a business model that concentrates on heavyweight problems (fractured bones, organ failures, infectious diseases, etc.) and provides major solutions (transplants, surgeries, antivirals, etc.) in response. There are solid monetary reasons for doing so, but the value in tackling micro-events—the daily or digitally silent event stream I mentioned throughout Part I, typically involving nutrition, sleep, exercise, and so on—remains too difficult to actually turn a profit.

In response to employer and payer demand, various clinics and medical practices have added specialists to focus on *proactive wellness*. The results have not been dramatic. In fact, research suggests employee wellness programs commonly fail to achieve the results they were designed to deliver.[46] The reasons vary and include issues related to low employee adoption, a lack of sustained engagement, uncertainty or even distrust in the way those delivering the service quantify certain results, and a lack of say in governance or control over data use.

In reality, as a society we have not realized the cost savings that proactive wellness programs promise. Is the health adjustment or health value too small to be impactful to either the individual or the sponsor?

Successful wellness programs involve the management of important (albeit mundane) decisions and micro-events. Here, the business model and focus flip: perhaps 10 percent better sleep is not enough to change the productivity of a single employee, but 10 percent better sleep across an entire population of one thousand employees is likely to be noticeable.

We are awash with technology that could enable the data streams to manage the micro-contributions of individuals while also generating a picture of population health. In doing so, we can go beyond *normal* and begin to define *optimal* for individuals and larger populations. Furthermore, personalized incentive structures would go a long way to producing more sustained engagement as people uncover their own progress in both health and economic benefit.

The bottom line: suggesting that a step-tracking program is "good for your health" is far too low a value proposition for most of our population. It will take a more nuanced understanding of diverse motivations in order to bend the adoption curve upward and sustain it over time. This is not something a corporate executive team can figure out. Only those on the ground with personal experiences have the ability to see the hidden realities of daily challenges. Until now, individuals have lacked the tools to self-organize and co-design locally relevant programs that are nimble enough to learn and evolve according to the groups they serve. Health intelligence is due for a serious reinvention checkpoint.

TODAY'S HEALTH INTELLIGENCE IS PLAGUED WITH GAPS

Most TV commercials for medical therapies include an "ask your doctor" suggestion, as if our personal physicians understand our unique needs across all therapeutic domains. In reality, few of us have a personal physician—more and more, we accept care from whichever app or practitioner is filling in at the local clinic or urgent care setting. Medical records, if they are available at all, are patchy, and information on various options are based on study populations. Thus, the information we receive is not entirely personally relevant. It comes with gaps and holes.

Just think about the questions that surface daily while trying to manage personal care pathways:

- *Should I have personalized laboratory targets?* Phil's father died at forty-eight with heart disease. What lipid levels should Phil target between his teens and his early forties to avoid his father's outcome?
- *What side effects will I experience?* Roger was prescribed a statin to lower his lipid levels. He is expected to take this medication for decades. How reversible would any muscle weakness, liver disease, diabetes, or the other potential long-term side effects be, should they show up for Roger?
- *What combination of care would be best for me?* Sandra had a hip replacement and wants to get back to her regular weekly tennis matches. Treadmill? Hiking? Yoga? Weights? What combination will ensure the quickest rehab?
- *Why are my medications so expensive?* Olive is a student and isn't managing her Type II diabetes well. Many young adults like Olive, who bounce in and out of insurance coverage, share insulin to cover gaps. Her vial may cost upward

of $300, even though the bill of materials may sit at roughly $26. Billing practices are hidden from those they affect most.

- *Why can't we get up-to-the-minute information?* Francis is four months out from her COVID-19 diagnosis. Daily, she still deals with brain fog, aches and pains, and fatigue. She has been extra careful with her diet and is exercising as recommended. Surely there must be something else she can do to start to feel better.

These scenarios result, at least in part, from the fact that health systems control our data. At best, we're allowed to visit it. In fact, we routinely hand our data over to central authorities: electronic medical record providers, health insurance companies, and so on. What's worse, we simply accept this as being a part of normal life, leaving ourselves with no control over the many pass-on-data business models that occur without our knowledge, consent, or involvement.

Consider the following two use cases, one involving a mother and daughter, the other a relatively healthy middle-aged man.

MACIE AND DARLENE

After her divorce, Macie's mother, Darlene, came to live with her to help look after her two young children. Within the first year, Darlene, who had been living with Type I diabetes since she was a teen, suffered a significant myocardial infarction.

Such an event isn't atypical for people in her situation. Darlene spent many months in cardiac rehab and struggled to look after herself over the next few years. She continued to live with Macie and the children, but their roles reversed. Macie kindly cared for her mother until Darlene's passing.

Like all children, Macie hadn't wanted her mother's health span during her last years to just be average. She wanted her mom to have had the best possible life for someone living with Type I diabetes and to have been able to stay as active as possible with her grandchildren.

Darlene's cohort, of course, falls into a normal distribution, with the vast majority in the middle and relatively few achieving better health for longer periods than others. Could Darlene have been an outlier? What would it have taken? How could Macie have known what might be reachable for her mother, given her situation, in time to make a difference? Was it in fact *reachable* to delay her heart attack by five, or perhaps ten, years? Might she have had access to detailed directives capable of delaying this outcome by a decade or more? How can we know?

Within the reality of web2, Macie and Darlene had no way of answering these questions. In an ideal world, it should be easy to scan the experiences of many thousands of people who had similar life paths, complete with an entire spectrum of health outcomes. Doing so would have provided a personalized *reachability management* to each of us as individuals. Like Darlene, and as with Troy from Part I, life is too complicated to get it right by ourselves. Healthcare as we know it is *reactive*—it provides too little, too late for many of us.

MATT

Matt is one of over three hundred thousand individuals per year who find themselves undergoing a total hip replacement (THR) in the US.[47] Matt learned as much as he could about hip replacement surgery, but a few weeks after surgery, he began to accept that his outcome was not what he had expected.

Today, standard electronic health records connect individuals to a select few of their personal providers: surgeon, family physician, and occasionally a physical therapist. However, not connected are the hundreds of thousands of individuals and practitioners that share a history of this experience.

Like them, Matt lacks access to meaningful incentives or a simple user interface that might encourage him to self-track his personal health journey. Instead, other entities will spread his medical images, laboratory data, physical therapy data, and more across different health delivery systems. He remains oddly on standby, waiting to be told when to visit his provider, when to walk more, and when to expect pain to diminish.

None of us can afford to get things wrong when it's time to undergo a significant mechanical adjustment such as a THR. Clearly there is a spectrum of health outcomes for any procedure. Some patients do well, others less so. Because THR is often an elective procedure, some patients are fortunate enough to orchestrate as preferred an outcome as possible. Still, on a large scale, we do not possess technology that supports a proactive understanding of our health futures in time to navigate deliberately toward the best outcomes.

Surely three hundred thousand individual THR experiences could have collectively provided strong correlations regarding which attributes tracked with the best outcomes. Armed with the collective reality of many, would Matt have been able to predict this outcome? Would he have been able to see around the corner sufficiently to course-correct in some small or large way?

The promise of big data is not new; non-healthcare industries have blazed a trail that sees around the corner of our purchasing behaviors. They proactively ensure we are purchasing *correctly* and without delay.

In a perfect world, Matt would have secure access to the data needed to drive personally relevant health decisions while being protected against the use of data for pure advertising or marketing. We are not there yet.

CHAPTER FIVE

IS RETAIL HEALTH THE ANSWER?

We remain stuck in an old mode of being visitors to our own personal data, in part because robust business interests and systems have rarely (if ever) been good at transformation. How long can healthcare, an industry that makes up almost 20 percent of US gross domestic product (GDP), remain unchanged?

Market sizes of this magnitude are hard to hide. Retail giants are envisioning and acting to secure a role in providing non-complex immediate care to communities. Of note, Amazon purchased One Medical, a concierge primary care service. One Medical has locations in areas with mostly young and affluent individuals. They charge a $200 annual fee and connect with patients using text and tele-visits as well as traditional in-person clinic visits.

What does this mean for traditional healthcare? There was a time that just holding medical records was enough to ensure customers returned for follow-on visits. Business-friendly patient lock-in could be assured by avoiding the sharing of medical records between institutions. What happens now? Will more user-friendly, convenient on-demand and mostly online care impact profits of the legacy players? History suggests that traditional healthcare, like the once brick-and-mortar bookstores, have much to fear.

Then there are us, the people: What rights do we have in this transaction? Though convenience may improve, the underlying data power asymmetry has yet to be adjusted. Amazon has access to a multitude of micro-events that are not recorded inside of our medical records. Does this mean Amazon can bypass the Health Insurance Portability and Accountability Act (HIPAA), which requires encounter data to lose various identifiers before it leaves and is mixed with data from other sites? Will my One Medical data immediately co-exist for exploration with my purchasing behaviors? Is the individual locked into an Amazon / One Medical model because they own and control her data?

Wait—there is one key reason to be optimistic!

Never have the incentives been so well aligned. Healthcare doesn't fare better financially when crowd health is optimized. Amazon is different, very different. Half of US households have an Amazon Prime account. Amazon cannot afford the kind of fat, depressed, and bankrupt populations the US healthcare system has produced.[48] No, most retail giants would prefer swarms of healthy folks with ever-expanding purchasing power. Could an era of mass participation in new data marketplaces provide an irresistible leap in personal finances and drive unprecidented purchasing behavior?

Will Prime Health be the route to SSI and personally controlled data streams? Clearly there is the cash here to build something profoundly different. In a web3 ownership model, patient-controlled data streams would essentially remove the need for lock-in. Amazon providers might benefit from a more robust stream of new patients seeking care if patients carried their own data. Moreover, new patients complete with clinically relevant data would drop onboarding requirements, minimize repeat questionnaires, and avoid redundant lab testing. Personally controlled health data could be a win-win for patients, providers, and retailers.

Another advantage of shifting much of the data procurement and management to the community includes the ability of healthcare organizations to offload significant risk. Personal health information, managed within personal health data systems, would augment the types of centralized storage we know today. Imagine robust safety and flexibility of distributed storage, ensuring individuals can provide access to their personal health data during visits to any health provider—regardless of where they are on the globe.

In short, while retail and traditional healthcare players jockey for position in this massive 20 percent of GDP market, creating new value in the form of new knowledge may continue to be hamstrung by web2 data practices. However, if this jockeying results in an injection of serious cash into transforming the industry along a web3 ownership economy ethos, our preferred futures may begin to unfold.

What's more, security, privacy, auditability, and new, nimble incentive models via NFTs could be built leveraging web3 tech. The result would allow us to self-organize and define what is *reachable* in terms of health expression in highly personalized and defined ways, thereby supporting whichever pathway a person should choose. Natural medicine? Yes. Eastern approach? Absolutely. High-performance athlete? Yes again. New pathways would be the result of new marketplaces for personal health information, which would enable data as an economic asset for all participants.

Sounds innovative, except it's not really—businesses regularly use data to expose reachability. A well-known app has provided reachability for years. Can you think of one?

ENTER: REACHABILITY MANAGEMENT

The notion of reachability management is not a new one. Consider Strava, a mobile platform for tracking activities on your phone. Strava provides a form of reachability management and boasts millions of new members each month. While not a perfect analog to the possibilities of web3, Strava does make an interesting use case.

If you're not familiar, here's a quick overview: Stella and her cycling friends have downloaded Strava on their phones to log their rides. Strava records their location, distance, and speed, and highlights any improvements they achieve. Stella has access to a longitudinal record of her rides over time, and she can see how well others have performed on the same sections of her rides.

In this way, Strava provides reachability information for its users. Stella can see the times of other riders, some identified as those she follows, and others that remain anonymous. In short, individuals that have ridden the same section and used the app to share their details define their performance. Taken together, rider data shares what is effectively reachable.

Imagine a web3 Strava-like model where users could combine personal training habits (sleep, nutrition, injury prevention exercises, etc.), a marketplace in which purchasing the verified event streams that underpin peak performance would be possible. The co-occurrences that align with outlier achievement are likely to be of interest to both the casual and the professional rider, but currently there is no marketplace or personal control of a user's riding data within the Strava experience.

While medical professionals seem to have little optimism when it comes to prescribing exercise to populations, the Centers for Disease Control and Prevention (CDC) recommends thirty minutes of exercise five times per week for the entire US adult population.[49] Given the technology available today, we should expect a more customized approach. What about personally relevant activity recommendations, which the CDC could source and share according to specificities of our unique situation? How much activity should I achieve to avoid a breast cancer recurrence? Imagine if groups of women were able to ask and answer these questions by self-organizing and collaborating with new and effective digital environments.

We all need reliable and personally relevant answers to our queries. Keep in mind that the modernization of our lives has brought dumpster-loads of suboptimal choices: cheeseburgers dripping with fat, supersized fast-food meals, quart-sized gulps of soda, and prepackaged sweets at every turn that have little to no resemblance to farm foods.

Does this mean humans are expected to use sensors and other devices that track our every move and guide us to smart health choices? Certainly not. There are graveyards full of wireless health tech that had hoped to do just that. Many are synonymous with life-logging, while doing little more than reflecting a user's data back at them.

Some medical experts feel validated when health apps fail. They argue that change is too hard for people—even those who start to make healthy lifestyle changes rarely sustain them. They say privacy is a deal-breaker and people will not share their health data.

Yet Strava and others are setting the groundwork for success. Imagine, within a web3 ownership economy, groups of people relying on *Strava*-sleep, for instance. This tool provides users with sleep data within the context of millions of other people from across the globe. When a user is desperate to feel less fatigue, like Stella, who had COVID-19 for a long period of time, they can use tokens to tap into the wisdom of all of the many Long COVID-19 individuals. They can then see who has succeeded in cobbling together a patchwork of remedies that, when taken together, seem to make a significant difference.

With reliable access to the successful co-occurrences, Stella can select those that might work for her: cohort-specific sleep supplements at night and a new routine during the day (short bursts of caffeine alternating with sports-recovery electrolytes and muscle stretching exercises for a few minutes every hour if she is stuck at her desk all day). Add a standing desk, and soon, with the help of her crowd, Stella achieves success over a once relentless fatigue.

This combination of contributors might have taken months or

years to figure out on our own. Together, no experience is too small. A continuous AI can learn without forgetting the tiniest detail. As such, remedies that are not contributory or, worse, carry harm are identified in a timely manner.

The more we share with each other, the more we can begin to learn which specific efforts are likely to work best for us. Business intelligence analyzes hundreds of thousands of inputs daily—not just on the hour, but on the minute—in order to ensure a sustainable future.

In health, the attributes that matter most span all domains of human functioning: nutrition, activity, sleep, social engagement, purposeful living, and many more. Crowd health expression is hugely valuable to individuals, businesses, and communities. Until recently, it has been difficult to access, analyze, and leverage the wisdom inherent in diverse human health expressions. With the spread of nonintrusive health-tracking devices and federated learning, we can begin to make sense of large digitized representations of the ebb and flow of health across communities.

Looking into the future, this type of collaborative push may become a fundamental requirement for delivering better pharmaceutical results. In the past, pharma would seek out a single biological target, develop a payload to deliver to that target, and hopefully generate a clinically relevant outcome. This narrow-scope approach has basically tapped out. Single targets do not work well, and biology is far too complex for the industry to stay in this lane.

The quest is on to achieve multi-targeted approaches: to understand resilience and define the parameters that dictate the emergence of future health events. Much more than focusing on Electronic Medical Record data alone, this will require understanding highly contextual and person-specific attributes that predate the onset of illness.

Using web3 approaches, the once unknowable for pharma may indeed become specifically permissioned—and therefore knowable. Still, getting the crowd to participate will take new standards of protecting privacy and security, as well as incentives, such as economic benefits, that make it hard to resist.

Individuals, industry, and healthcare must recognize their deep interdependencies within our free-living system: the flows of information, energy, and matter, which determine our human condition. Only together can we maximize our collective health and economic futures. Crowds safely collaborating in and between various data marketplaces can uncover biological truths and more. Collective data-driven insights can help uncover discrepancies in billing across procedures, bias in testing, and unexpected rates of misdiagnosis.

Before our aspirations exceed our ability to deliver, let's stay aligned to a few basic questions:

- What will the tech look like?
- How will it work?
- Why should we expect privacy and security will be any better than what we're used to?
- How will a culture of mistrusting strangers shift to one in which we are comfortable accessing and learning from others' lived experiences while offering our data-driven insights back to the crowd?

Imagine a world where all of your health data is available to you, regardless of where you are on the globe. Cycling in Italy with a newly sprained ankle—the same ankle you fractured five years ago—your X-rays might be hard to interpret without earlier images for comparison. No worries. With a couple of taps, your earlier images are available for review by an Italian clinician, without anything being lost in translation. Just the convenience and peace of mind knowing you're fully connected to your health data sounds magnificent. Shouldn't this be a universal right of sorts?

BurstIQ, one of many blockchain services companies, provides the following starter set of principles addressing the rights of citizens:

- We should own our data.
- We should have access to all our data.
- We should have confidence that our data is safe.
- We should be able to trust and understand our data.
- We should be able to control who can access our data.
- We should be able to help society with our data.[50]

This set of principles is easily stated, yet not as easily delivered, given our current state of affairs. Industry no longer needs to hold and manage our individual data elements via centralized web2 approaches. This antiquated process limits our access to full intelligence, which in turn limits the health and economic benefit that we can achieve. We no longer need to be locked into yesterday's assumptions. Conventional wisdom and scientific discovery are due for a serious upgrade. Together, people with shared goals can use a parallel system of digital health rails to deliver personally relevant intelligence while supporting new marketplaces that benefit all: citizens, industry, and retailers alike. In Part III, we'll go deeper into this new set of rails.

PART III

INSIGHTS, ZONES, AND MAKING IT WORK

CHAPTER SIX

GETTING THERE: A THREE-ZONE APPROACH

You never change things by fighting the existing reality. To change something, build a new model that makes the existing model obsolete.

—BUCKMINSTER FULLER

To be clear, the goal here is to provide a new data model that corrects our current power asymmetry, leads to patient-centric care, and makes parts of our existing data model obsolete. Why do this? Because doing so has the potential to advance human health expression, as well as capital outcomes, for participants.

A recent article by the economist Glenn Hubbard reminds us that the limits of capitalism actually threaten its existence as a preferred economic structure.[51] Capitalism is measured, in part, by how effective it is in lifting the average wage. Average is not a good target to measure. Outsized advances in terms of the highest wage earners will also lift the average wage. Meanwhile, large portions of our population remain left out of any benefit. Hubbard's key message: a capitalist society should boost productive potential by building and maintaining broad infrastructure to support an open economy that advances the ability of all citizens and communities to both contribute and compete.

A parallel argument can be made in health. Average health is not optimal health. If the average survival post–stage IV cancer is two years, is this enough? Who are the outliers that achieved remarkable remissions? How and why were these remissions possible? Traditional search engines don't help us here as they lack the training data. In an ideal world, the specific details or co-occurrences associated with the best outcomes would be available. Each of us, regardless of the diagnosis, would have a solid shot at ignoring average and deliberately designing an outlier achievement.

Recall Troy from Part I? His group may be blindly and passively shifting in the wrong direction and moving below average. Without effort, children may find themselves without the skills and achievements that came relatively accidentally to their parents. Even with reasonable genetic material, Troy's group lives in a new paradigm. With altered activity and nutrition, this group may achieve much less than their parents. Some experts suggest that children of Troy's generation, and the generations that follow, may be more likely to die at a younger age than their parents than preceding generations; in the very least, they are primed to suffer the consequences of a shorter health span (number of life years without illness).[52]

Today, web2 data models continue to make it easy for large companies to own value and deliver average to populations. A web3 ownership economy offers a broad technical infrastructure that seeks to expand the limits of traditional capitalism. It promises to help advance the ability of citizens and communities to contribute and compete. The fundamental difference that's responsible for a more robust form of capitalism is the web3-enabled shift to personally owned data assets and greater individual economic participation. From that perspective, web3 can best be defined as leading a tectonic shift in ethos and culture.

At the same time, web2 will not become obsolete. Instead, web3 will provide a new set of rails, giving users more choices: pursue capitalism according to what you currently know, or take advantage of options that are nimbler and easier to scale. The promises remain tantalizing, to say the least: web3 may provide more digitally native, software-based companies that open the floodgates to massive collaboration to achieve common goals; it may produce an era where, with less effort, less capital, and more flexibility, we can achieve greater wealth than what we know today; we may be able to learn faster, with higher specificity, and co-produce more wealth than was ever possible before.

Again, these are promises, and fairly broad ones at that. How do we get there? What are the micro-steps we must follow?

More than anything, let's come back to the fact that we should all enjoy ownership of our digital footprint, regardless of where we choose to walk. We should own our social content: words, photos, videos, and so on. We should own our transactions: financial, educational, and health related. Via web3, we can gain access to a broad infrastructure that supports an open economy and permits each of us to compete for better knowledge, health, and wealth—one that helps individuals and communities move beyond *average* and begin to achieve *optimal* results.

Within the underpinnings of web3 health, we find a tech stack, leveraging blockchain-based data structures, that supports mass flourishing without necessarily disrupting traditional healthcare—expect new rails without dismantling the old ones. In fact, web3 health provides a new set of rails that pick up where capitalism has fallen short, much like Bitcoin offers a new set of rails where traditional finance has fallen short.

As detailed by Mike Roth, partner at ManyUses and previously a co-founder and the chief technology officer at Radar Relay, a web3 future

> is one in which all data, including our identities, is self-sovereign and kept secure. High-quality information flows freely and to the benefit of its originators in perpetuity—in this regard, that would be us, the users. Inefficiencies and ecological misalignments no longer exist in our financial, logistics, healthcare, governance, and commerce systems. Most importantly, it's where we balance the scales of luck (genes, geography, inheritance) with meritocracy so that hard work and determination can change your destiny no matter what your background might be.[53]

Recall the use case for Matt in Part II, who had a total hip replacement and whose recovery was less than average? If a web3 future could have changed Matt's destiny, what might it have looked like? While clearly detailed technical specifications are slightly beyond the scope of this book, what follows is a proposal of a simple three-zone model to highlight the key attributes of a web3 tech stack for the future of healthcare.

Zone I: Homebase—personal data streams stored, organized, and with terms of use for follow-on opportunities

Zone II: Federated Correlation AI—a secure means of querying a homebase along with others to expose clinically relevant truths

Zone III: Commercial—marketplaces leverage correlations exposed in Zone II and co-create new value while ensuring rewards accrue in perpetuity to the originators of each micro-contribution to the new value and products

In the pages that follow, we'll walk through these zones with the help of a young man named Adam and break things down into specific details. After our walk-through, we'll turn our attention to a young girl named Truun. Note that unlike our previous use cases, Adam's and Truun's stories take place in this envisioned future. As you read, I invite you to take this slight leap of faith as we flash forward to a few years from now.

ADAM

To start, Adam has been accumulating his health data inside of a homebase: his personal health record. The health data paradigm he follows within web3 promises to allow him—as well as our future selves—to leverage personal homebase records with federated learning to support greater health intelligence, as well as robust, new smarter marketplaces.

As Adam goes through a hip replacement, we'll track his experience according to the following:

- **Zone I:** Adam's homebase, which includes his longitudinal personal health information
- **Zone II:** A benevolent, non-rivalrous federated learning AI layer that uncovers key correlations related to his situation
- **Zone III:** A commercial zone (the medical-industrial complex) that provides Adam with targeted health opportunities that are more specific to his situation than anything any of us are privy to in web2

ZONE I

Whenever Adam visits a clinic or hospital, his phone provides his self-sovereign identity (SSI) QR code to ensure that whatever data the clinic gathers during his visit goes into his Zone I data pod. For Adam, as for all of us in the web3 structure, there are no geographic borders to Zone I. People from all walks of life, and most corners of the earth, participate by accumulating personal health data within their homebase. Regulations, if any, are remarkably light. Privacy, security, and personal choice are largely *baked in* via blockchain-based smart contracts.

Adam's homebase has pointers to extra-large medical files, including images and device interrogations, located in multiple distributed storage containers. These aspects of his digital health identity are not locked inside patient portals or controlled by entities like Google, United Health, Apple, or any other large player. He owns them, and they are available to Adam regardless of where he goes, no matter which clinic or provider he visits. This creates a seamlessness of medical and health support unlike anything we currently know.

In addition, because these elements of Adam's digital health record are tied to his SSI, other parties cannot access or share them without his explicit consent. Using the power of block-chain and smart contracts operating under his control, Adam's information is remarkably tamper-proof. Audits are built in, and the notion of a data breach becomes highly improbable, if not obsolete.

ZONE II

Zone II provides for easy access to the health expression of many and, as such, uncovers correlations that might matter at the pace of change. Adam, like many others, defaults portions of his data to be available to the federated correlation AI in Zone II. With hundreds of thousands of procedures preceding his own, Adam is able to use the federate correlation tool to query the homebase records of other people—without revealing any personally identifying information—in order to uncover the attributes most associated with best outcomes. Adam regularly permits access to his own homebase for contextual information. He receives tokens for sharing and uses accumulated tokens to run his own queries, mostly free of charge, in return.

Relevant context data (e.g. step count, activity intensity and duration, pain scores with exertion and at rest, the use of over-the-counter or prescription medication) all contribute to a more meaningful understanding of the drivers responsible for preferred health experiences. Adam's data benefits others, while their data benefits him.

For all of us, Zone II is a completely noncommercial, intellectual property-free zone. Basic federated AI runs by the people, for the people, on demand, to serve up potential correlations.

Clearly correlations are not causations; however, a web3 health data model ensures *high-quality information flows freely* to offer clues regarding a plethora of personally relevant products and services.

Having access to the health expression of patients that went before may produce sufficient insights to direct *hard work and determination, which might change our destiny*. For instance, Adam discovers a lot about hip pain and THR prior to his surgery using key correlations, and he puts this to good use with the help of options he finds in the commercial Zone III layer (which will explore in greater detail shortly).

- He researches orthopedic facilities and provider names, along with costs and outcomes, and gains confidence that his surgeon will be a good fit.
- He is able to find detailed recommendations regarding protocols to optimize his lean body mass and fitness levels prior to surgery.
- He optimizes sleep habits using a tool similar to the Oura Ring (a sleep- and activity-tracking device that reads heart rate and other vitals via your index finger).
- He rents a house in Sedona for four weeks post-op in order to walk the rocky and irregular trails rather than use the smooth-surface treadmill at home.
- He purchases a NutriBullet blender and the ingredients he needs to make recommended post-operative shakes.
- He takes advantage of meditation, massage, and physiotherapy gems, all of which correlate with best outcomes.

Moving forward, Adam plans to put his data to work in hopes of generating a passive financial outcome for himself. His THR should not only generate optimal health function, but when combing real-world data streams surrounding this event, his THR should also generate optimal economic value. This comprehensive data stream, once tokenized and entered into various marketplaces, will return value to Adam in perpetuity. Furthermore, his data choices regarding privacy and control remain built-in parts of the vibrant ecosystem he uses, while trusted intermediaries (his personal digital fiduciaries) manage additional layers of flexibility.[54]

ZONE III

As the commercial layer, Zone III is where health industries and retailers access preapproved correlations to understand the ebb and flow of customer behaviors and related outcomes. Here, scientific rigor helps to uncover causal relationships with the use of industrial-grade federated learning. A continuous connection between Zones II and III enables dynamic learning that industry players can access and cross-reference with conditions on the ground.

A steady stream of real-world data generates more robust insights, helping these very same players produce and deliver more personally relevant products and services. In addition, this three-zone structure ensures that industry partners with citizens to co-produce new products and services. Successful markets scale, while economic benefits cycle back to individuals according to the value they provide via data insights. This ensures that new value benefits those who create and *willingly* share the data— people—in perpetuity, while the types of inefficiencies, biases, and misaligned incentives we experience in web2 fade. Here, we see the switch turn from previously average to new levels of optimal.

With the help of a digital fiduciary, Adam locates a number of data marketplaces that fit his criteria:

- A medical device company is recruiting patients for post-market surveillance data.
- A pharma company is looking for patients who are willing to provide views of baseline data and test a post-surgical sleep aid.
- A union of postal carriers is looking for people with THR experiences to discover the best therapeutic pathways for their co-workers.
- An offshore union of retired professional soccer players is purchasing THR insights from the US.

In Zone II, Adam, along with other citizens, uses simple query tools to determine if various environmental, personal, nutritional, and other co-occurrences are more or less associated with different outcomes. To see how these actions transition to Zone III, let's imagine that a pharma company wishes to track the prevalence of sleep difficulties associated with post-op care.

Using a federated learning approach, Adam's data and conditions for use remain secure within his personal homebase. The company's sleep query will present itself to Adam's conditions for use. Adam has control over what entities can and cannot access his information. Assuming he has given this type of query a green light, the following occurs:

- Adam receives tokens in exchange for his data.
- The pharmaceutical AI model gains access to read approved portions of Adam's homebase (Zone I), based on his preset criteria and share options.

- Using this information, the parameters of the AI model are updated.
- Various updates ensure the AI has been trained on diverse populations, as well as helping verify that predicted outcomes are aligned or corrected as needed to match those ultimately occurring in the field.

This federated learning model ensures that no entity can transport, remove, or make Adam's data available for unauthorized use. Each and every query is logged, and Adam has access and insight into who uses his data and for what purposes.

On the wealth-creation side of the equation, Adam accumulates tokens for making his data available—a *share-to-earn* approach. Adam can use his tokens to fund future queries and pay for various products and services. By participating in global data marketplaces, Adam gains economic benefit and also gathers insights from individuals with diverse cultures and living conditions.

Among the correlations Adam discovers during this experience is that many individuals share similar sleep challenges. He used to only get five hours of sleep per night. However, using the personally directed federated learning, Adam successfully tinkers with his routine and now regularly achieves an extra ninety minutes of sleep each night.

Beyond putting this data to work for his own benefit, Adam uses his tokens to fund follow-on services that manage participation in appropriate Zone III marketplaces. These services can use pseudonyms to ensure optimal de-identification while still tracking transparency and accountability with regards to data use within marketplaces.

High-end services provide a trusted intermediary (digital fiduciary, which can be a person, a personal AI, or a combination of the two) to work on Adam's behalf. His fiduciary scans data-purchasing opportunities in Zone III according to Adam's search criteria. Together, Adam's terms of use and his fiduciary match a buyer's smart contract terms with levels of access to Adam's data.

For example, a specified set of preferred research institutions benefit from automatic data contributions. These institutions meet all criteria, including follow-on payment requirements. Adam's fiduciary interfaces to interpret data requests and manage transaction ledgers so that income (via tokens) covers the costs of service and provides Adam with additional passive funds.

The personal fiduciary model may evolve to source and integrate other services for Adam, many of which will be automated as a personal AI, including things like:

- Scanning for unsolicited advertising and other attention-consuming materials
- Blocking facial-recognition tech when Adam has not given user authorization
- Keeping Adam's name from being added to address lists or any other unauthorized use of his contact info or identity
- Providing roll-up periodic reporting, such as the number of spam blocked or number and types of requests for data (enabled or otherwise)
- Comparing his personal data practices with those of other people in order to detect ways in which Adam can further optimize his data management for personal or community benefit

In the web3 model that Adam knows, traditional healthcare regulatory conditions cover Zone III activities, yet, thanks to better built-in audits, compliance is more enforceable than what we know in web2. Safe to say, we've learned a lot about the properties that enable various power imbalances that plague our current online existence. Will it be possible to engineer a future that adequately protects us from deteriorating back to the commercial practices we know today? Can we truly build such a robust business value that sliding backward makes no financial sense? The answer may rest on Zone III's use of data pools.

Not all data unions are commercial in nature. Some provide participation for collective benefit within nonmonetary structures. Others, commercial data pools or unions, apply data science methods, systematic studies, trials, and so on, the combination of which results in a new version of a trained model, which then spans across an individual's shared data. This creates robust and targeted commercial predictions, for instance, whether intervention X—surgery, a dietary change, a new workout regimen—will produce result Y. Indeed, there may be many models, since most commercial interests will tie their predictions to their own products or services.

In this case, it brings up two important considerations related to Zone III: Can people trust the answers they receive, or will they simply see a new version of web2's targeted advertising? And by giving individuals more control of their data, won't companies lose power?

Yakov Feygin, during a *Things Have Changed* podcast, interviewed Nick Vincent, whose work on power imbalances we discussed in Chapter 1.[55] Yakov reminds us that every minute, people swipe 990,000 Tinder profiles and send 156 million emails, plus another 16 million text messages. Meanwhile, Google processes 40,000 searches a second and 1.4 billion people log into Facebook/Meta every day. We live in a digital economy, and it runs on data. With the digital-ad-revenue business estimated at a whopping $200 billion, addressing whether or not it's possible to balance the scales between data providers (us) and data brokers (the personal data industry) is a worthwhile question.

Vincent provides a framework for reshaping our current data power distribution.[56] He advocates for organizations that profit from our data to *pay a share* of those earnings to the data originators. Others are taking action as well. Andrew Yang, a former presidential candidate, launched a Data Dividend Project in 2020, which seeks to provide data ownership rights to individuals.[57]

Today, we walk into an examining room with little knowledge that the information we disclose carries financial value to third parties. Without any of us giving explicit permission, providers remove personal identifiers from our information, and the rest of our data hits the vast marketplace for businesses to purchase and repurpose for their own benefit.

It's widely assumed that HIPAA protects against other entities divulging our medical data. However, once personal identifiers disappear, HIPAA no longer applies protections. Typically, data-purchasing companies use machine learning and AI to loosely reattach identifying information to boost predictive capacity, but re-identification is not without error. For this reason and others, the data, while suitable for advertising and marketing purposes, does little for scientific discovery.

To recap in fairly blunt terms: without expressed permission, our private health concerns are being sold from underneath us, making their way to the marketplace every day. Very few of us, if any, would willingly provide private information in order to simply generate more advertising if given the choice. We would rather see our information go toward meaningful scientific discovery and medical breakthroughs. Unfortunately, the mechanics of working within HIPAA regulations generates data quality significantly suited for marketing rather than scientific discovery.

To some, the three-zone scenario painted above, with the help of Adam's journey, may seem improbable. Comprehensive personal health data from multiple providers available at any time with just a tap on our phone? Passive income while enjoying robust privacy and security? A personal digital fiduciary? Will we see a widening of the digital divide?

Let's switch gears and glimpse into the life of Truun, a child of the web3 future. In the process, we'll return to a number of the terms first introduced in the Primer section.

TRUUN

Before Truun's birth, her parents, Liz and Louis, log their pregnancy journey on their longitudinal health records (Zone I). They are both part of a DAO for home births (Zone III), and as such, they buy tokens known as HBTs (home-birth tokens) and are part of a co-op DAO model that helps members manage and support the financial needs for home-birth families. The token economics within this DAO work like this:

- Every ten-dollar purchase of HBT is split immediately:
    - 70 percent goes to the user
    - 10 percent goes to support Zone II
    - 10 percent goes to a pool of funds to cover unexpected costs (hospital visit, unplanned C-section, blood transfusion, etc.)
    - 5 percent is burned to offset the ten-dollar purchase[58]
    - 5 percent is shared across all HBT holders[59]

HBT holders can purchase or earn additional tokens by providing laboratory data, wearable device data (activity/sleep trackers and so on), pregnancy stories (good as well as less optimal outcomes), prices paid for services (price transparency), lists of health markers tracked by their providers (to help avoid provider bias), photos, videos, and other content to the collective. Credentialed users can earn HBTs by hosting nutrition webinars and providing checklists and other tools to the community.

The world at the time of Truun's birth is one in which advanced automation has taken over many aspects of employment. The gig economy dictates that families are in and out of employer-sponsored health coverage. Couples going through a pregnancy use this data market option to ensure a financial safety net for unexpected expenses. Participants gain passive income as other users purchase access to checklists, recipes, and other creative content specific to their pregnancy needs. NFTs ensure that the content creators gain any economic lift produced via their contributions in perpetuity.

Members of the DAO vote on many decisions—in fact, the DAO's governance depends on distributed participation. DAO members determine aspects such as:

- Token allocations to purchasing correlations from Zone II
- Selling data to other Zone III industries
- Defining pregnancy-related events that resources help to fund
- Sharing economic benefits from updating algorithms to ensure their predictive capacity remains optimized within an ever-changing human behavior landscape

In addition, insight from members of the DAO provides quality control and oversight of practitioners and practices via continuously updating the community data commons. This also helps create a massive lift in human intelligence specific to pregnancy. In fact, each future birth benefits from every birth that came before. Nothing is lost. By and large, families, single mothers, and practitioners avoid the mistakes of the past.

- Prior to labor, Zone II provides correlations that sort out hundreds of patterns of vague pregnancy symptoms. When is pregnancy-related fatigue clinically concerning?
- Practitioners scan the ebb and flow of heart rate and temperature across hundreds of presentations in order to catch potential bacterial infections. This helps to avoid premature birth outcomes.
- Pregnant women receive personally relevant recommendations about diet and activity rather than mostly *winging it*.
- Practitioners recognize breech presentations and other issues in time to manage appropriately.

- No longer does one size fit all. Target gestation is not forty weeks for everyone. With improved pregnancy dating and accounting for clinically relevant contributors, some cohorts fall into the thirty-eight-weeks-plus-five-days gestation group. Late-pregnancy stillbirths are avoided. Personalized gestation targets are specific for a host of meaningful attributes.
- High-definition, personally relevant understanding accompanies each couple into each stage of their pregnancy.
- Once a child arrives, new moms and families can find social support and locally pooled childcare.

Via user permissions, in addition to voting, the DAO sells packages of data to industry. The people within the DAO, including Liz and Louis, control what data is available for purchase, under what conditions and for what price, at all times. In practice, they automatically set these stakes using thresholds that match individual personality types, but users can manually adjust them at any time. To a large degree, this helps solve preventable cost burdens for employers, who have long seen pregnancies as significant line items. Now, part of certain employee benefits plans include HBT options. Payers rely on the steady stream of real-world data to update clinically relevant thresholds, which are critical for safely managing labor and delivery.

Once Truun is born, and after Liz and Louis have gone through what feels like a fairly standard postpartum experience, the couple decides to cash out their HBT and put their HBT status on standby. Baby Truun receives her SSI, and her parents begin managing her longitudinal health record. To start, they make sure it is loaded with all of her prenatal, natal, and postnatal information to date. Throughout Truun's childhood, they can use this data as necessary, as can Truun once she comes of age.

Having cashed out her HBT tokens, Liz uses the proceeds to purchase early childhood tokens (ECTs). By this time, early preschool is available to all; however, Zone II correlations have highlighted that preschool alone is at best a half solution regarding childhood development. Developing brains are masses of specialized nervous tissue. They require specific structural inputs or building blocks in order to generate brain tissue capable of complex math and science.

In fact, Liz's research on the Zone II layer confirms that children who achieve high computational skills later in life require nutritional and behavioral building blocks from the start: plenty of fish and vegetables in their diet, competitive play and activity, and good-quality sleep, if possible. In this regard, Truun, unlike Troy from Part I, could have a direct line to her full genetic potential, as Liz and Louis access crowd-generated thresholds that relate to high-yield childhood outcomes.

In other words, Truun's parents have nimble and personally relevant access to the event streams that predate achievements for large numbers of youth. This comprehensive look at what works and what doesn't provides the opportunity to ensure their daughter will reach what is truly reachable—optimal—given her genetic disposition, home life, and social conditions. Truun's parents, like many in this era, will continue to rely on the health expression of crowds of children from across the globe to inform what is reachable for any specific moment and time. These thresholds update continuously on account of a steady stream of Zone II correlations, which then feed back into highly personalized and creative tools that offer Truun and many children of her generation various tracks to choose from.

Truun's medical visits are very different from Troy's, a one-time complete physical in his early twenties that uncovered an unexpected maturation through puberty. She shares a small nonintrusive but steady data stream of high-yield health contributors with her various health practitioners (both automated and analog) within various services (Western medicine, Chinese health, female health services, etc.). Rather than booking appointments according to age, Truun tracks progress along crowd-based continuums. Periodically, data trends prompt her practitioner to recommend a complete checkup, but this is not the old thirty-minute appointment with a health professional. Instead, Truun receives a package of extra sensors and instructions for specific events:

- Six-minute walk with twenty stairs
- Ten-minute run, flat plus hills
- Spine and limb range of motion and strength exercises
- Six packets of test nutrition with postconsumption blood sugar and other labs
- Enhanced sleep recording

The entire enhanced data stream is likely to require a few days to complete (perhaps close to two weeks to amplify the data stream prior to visiting with her practitioner). Most basic lab tests are collected at home, while more specialized testing takes place while Truun visits practitioners in physical settings.

All data streams port to Truun's homebase and are available

for correlation AI in Zone II. Truun accepts the extra hassle of enhancing her data streams for periodic representative high definition of her health trajectory. She knows her health value and economic opportunity jumps significantly with each check-in, and the payout is worth the effort. She has new ways to see around health corners and compare her achievements with those the crowd has defined as *reachable.*

Recall how Troy and his family had no idea that common event streams could coalesce to create educational, vocational, and social challenges in the future. In the three-zone future, con-sequential truths are *always on* and available to participants. In this way, Truun can learn early on that she may be at increased risk for breast cancer. By paying attention to those factors in her control and paying attention to screening options, she can actively reduce her risk to the lowest possible risk *reachable,* thanks to all the women that went before her.

Equally available to Truun is the option to ignore active breast cancer risk-reduction recommendations. However, because the information is provided at a time to make a difference, Truun and others like her, regardless of their personal choices, have the possibility of informed consent to their own health futures.

Informed consent is already part of the regulatory landscape of healthcare. But without widespread, safe, and secure data sharing across diverse populations, the *informed* part is a tiny fraction of what is *reachable* using web3 tech. This brings us to further consider the regulatory parameters that might underpin our preferred tomorrow.

CHAPTER SEVEN

SEPARATING ZONES BY REGULATORY PARAMETERS

This has always been one of those discussion points within the web: to what extent do we go sector by sector with regulation versus a single set of laws and regulations that apply across the board to all the players? What preexisting regulations make sense to adopt within the three-zone structure proposed above? Let's briefly consider each zone:

ZONE I: OUR PERSONAL HOMEBASE

We expect very little in the way of regulation other than the expressed right to have computational versions of our medical records default to our homebase. Just as HIPAA stays silent in regards to individual control of personal data, we expect to freely use our data for purposes that meet our needs and support our passions throughout the decades of our lives.

ZONE II: OUR AI/CORRELATION ZONE

A universal AI utility could be available to citizens as they accumulate health experiences onto their homebase. In this space, and without disclosing identity, people can query possible correlations that reflect their situation. These queries are executed using a federated learning model across all available and permissioned information in Zone I. Correlations are then available to any participant who is interested in them. There is no benefit to secrecy or exclusivity.

Still, a big question remains: Can we truly design a zone that remains noncommercial, non-rivalrous, open-source, and free of territorial intellectual property (IP) squabble? Ideally, Zone II allows information to flow freely, keeps identities fully cloaked, and provides people with access to AI queries on demand. Accomplishing these outcomes may be a heavy lift in a world where we are taught to build fences around our IP.

Adrian Gropper, CTO of Patient Privacy Rights, asserts that an IP-free zone is a fundamental property of Zone II.[60] This should resemble what happens in traditional medicine today. As people attend medical school, they absorb knowledge and skills, and we don't try to hide anything that might be important for health outcomes. When a radiologist locates a clinically relevant image on an X-ray that others might miss, the correct response is to write it up, not hoard or silo the information for personal gain; others can then discuss the films, and colleagues can gain insight into future cases. New knowledge spreads across medical fields in this way every day.

Now contrast the human clinician to a digital solution. Increasingly, algorithms prove to be exceptionally useful in scanning medical images for clinically relevant findings. These algorithms typically expect to file for IP protection. When our skills are digitized, thereby enabling IP lockdown, the situation becomes problematic.

Imagine a surgeon saying something to the effect of "My surgical procedure is secret. I'll only show you if you first sign the licensing agreement. And you can't ever modify it unless I have updated the license to permit a change." This level of secrecy does not exist in medical practice, nor do we see it in the regulatory system between those who have medical licenses and those of us that put products through the US Food and Drug Administration (FDA), with or without AI.

Drug companies work to secure IP because of outsized development costs, but this is an extremely limited situation. The bulk of medical knowledge should not, through digitization, become locked inside of IP. This is an ethical problem that needs to be sorted out. Limiting the sharing of knowledge would surely impact any advancing survival of our species.

ZONE III: OUR COMMERCIAL ZONE

This is where industry and providers step in and offer products, services, and support that correlate with our needs. Essentially, Zone III will carry a market regulatory framework similar to that which is in operation today, assuming necessary adjustments and improvements occur over time. Meanwhile, using tokens to track activities creates a new way for industry players to understand which market behaviors benefit the public versus those that may not.

DATA AND THE PATH TO SCIENTIFIC DISCOVERY

Human life as we know it is fragile and is changing at a pace with which traditional discovery cannot keep up. How can we address the power imbalance while still generating personally relevant scientific truths in time to make a difference? It's clear that the world would benefit from a more robust scientific discovery.

Today, many data companies refer to their extraction practices as simply harvesting data exhaust, suggesting it is basically a free and otherwise useless by-product of online behavior.[61] Clearly, the outsized revenue streams enjoyed by these companies confirm that so-called otherwise useless data exhaust may not at all be accurate vocabulary in this case.

The three-zone approach above proposes a framework that recognizes data production as data labor—a value-based opt-in that financially rewards people for the information they feed into the system. As the three-zone approach within the web3 framework, we will begin to see the rise of data unions as a means to extract an even more balanced power distribution.

Data unions might have sounded highly improbable a few years ago. Today, however, it is possible to envision a DAO as a data union of sorts. Consider the following scenario:

1. A group wants to map the cost and clinical outcomes for a specific diagnosis, such as breast cancer.
2. They decide to set up an online, fully virtual corporation that accepts conscious data contributions from an individual's Zone I homebase.
3. People contribute in the form of copies of their personal health. These copies are certified with regards to prove-

nance with an NFT, which acts as a unique identifier and a smart contract to oversee any migration into various data unions, as well as any future follow-on events.

Answering complex questions requires volumes of high-quality, diverse data to be interrogated. Data unions may well be a powerful way of combining value at scale. The authentic health experiences captured in our personal homebase can be permissioned to coexist with others in the pursuit of knowledge.

What's clear is that we can and must do much better with regards to health and health expression in the coming decades. It is also clear that optimal human health expression once depended upon ground conditions that no longer exist by default in modern societies. It's upon us to create new intelligence-gathering capabilities that allow us to pull together key ingredients in order to generate the best outcomes possible across the decades of our lives.

This is not an unrealistically optimistic scenario. In fact, these changes are already happening. The financial system is changing. Cannabis is also teaching populations the benefits of crowd collaboration and more. In Part IV, we explore the lessons from these and other industries that may already be showing the way forward.

THE FUTURE
IS DATA
OWNERSHIP

CHAPTER EIGHT

NOT *ACCESS* BUT *OWNERSHIP*, NOT *PRIVACY* BUT *PROPERTY*

Until recently, most regulations regarding data use have been discussed under the labels of privacy and access rights. Who can access data, and for what purposes? This may have been prudent years ago when asking individuals to own and manage their personal data would have been technically infeasible. Most patients avoided data discussions and assumed the hospital and clinic would look after their records on their behalf.

Today, we can no longer assume it would be unreasonable for people and families to manage their own health data. Technical advances and much-improved user experience has made it possible to provide simplicity and elegance to digital tools. This, in turn, has led to a growth in basic data literacy, as more and more people manage online banking, travel, and access to many other services via their phone or tablet. Clearly there are many benefits to a new attitude toward health data as personal property. For instance, when traveling, any mishaps that require medical attention would be simplified if people could access a medically verified reporting of underlying conditions and current medications.

Many people and families work with multiple providers at any given time (family practitioner, rheumatologist, dermatologist, physiotherapist, etc.), and these providers struggle with data silos—one practitioner is not aware of another's care plan, and vice versa. Without good access to this information, medical tests get duplicated and medication can interact, often with adverse effects. A single source of the truth, available from the patient to each practitioner, would go a long way to sorting out this tangled mess. A personal health record system would also make it easy to combine data from various sources: self-report, wearables, clinic visits, gym activities, nutritional consumption, and more.

If patients manage their personal health data, then health systems would not need to house thousands and sometimes millions of records within central storage locations, many of which are under constant threat from breaches and ransom attacks. The data would be distributed across individual storage solutions and thus much less attractive to bad actors.

This may all sound rather practical, and clearly there is a case to be made that data originating from our bodies must in some sense belong to us at the end of the day. Current laws regarding property already exist (to possess personal data, to use data as we please, to dispose of data as we please, and to generate personal value from the data), so a new legal framework may not be needed. If the technology is here to enable personal management of our data assets, then what is the holdup? Follow the money.

Though some states have presented bills to support personal health data as personal property, big business has pressured against this direction. It may come as a surprise that the American Civil Liberties Union (ACLU) is actively lobbying against health data as personal property. They cloak the argument in terms of "privacy, not property," which may be related to the fact that our ACLU received millions from Amazon, Facebook/Meta, Google, and others. These large players' business models depend on a steady stream of user data for which each of us is required to sign a *user agreement*: the fifty page-plus document that outlines how our privacy is *protected*...pages beyond our reading or comprehension. How can these agreements be legally binding if no one has actually read them?

To these big players and others, data as property is a problem. If I own an asset, then others would be required to seek my approval before they used said asset to generate revenues. The other cloak is research. Clearly we need to access data to advance science. However, as mentioned previously, this argument does not match up with the behemoth use of data for advertising revenue. As Adam Tanner details in his book *Our Bodies, Our Data: How Companies Make Billions Selling Our Medical Records*, companies make billions selling our medical records.[62]

Furthermore, if a data asset were used for research or other common goods (excluding revenue), it might be possible to design access to an asset without explicit approval. Cloaking the argument against property by suggesting large players have our back and provide meaningful privacy remains problematic. We continue to operate in a world where little to no permission is required.

Hopefully a strong argument for personal health data as property prevails in short order. Our citizenry is waking up to the power of ownership of digital assets as they engage in play-to-earn gaming, NFT transactions, and metaverse land grabs. Just as personal digital banking and travel plans have become part of everyday life, so too will health data ownership economies drive ever more revenue streams for business and individuals alike.

I believe that with web3 on the horizon, the possibilities of data ownership and meaningful sharing are indeed within reach. It starts with our Zone I homebase, which collects our digital content throughout the decades of our lives, hopefully without us having to do much more than opt in. This ensures that rich co-occurrence data will be time-stamped, traceable, and tamper-proof. The prevailing tech principles of this type of data ownership and stewardship will create many outcomes.

We will not be required to disclose our identity. Instead, we will have the discretion to do so when we choose. Personal and group queries may occur by the people, for the people, in an *always-on* fashion. Gaining knowledge and personally relevant insight will be the result of sharing our information.

At the Zone II layer, the AI will generate outcomes based on our personal scenario. To this end, the AI may weigh contributors differently or focus on high-yield co-occurrences that are uniquely relevant to us as individuals.

Data leverage and conscious data contributions will align with subscriptions and connections we might choose at the Zone III (commercial) level. In this way, we will be giving companies intentional, targeted, and secure access to rich correlations at the pace of change.

Finally, Zone III transactions will provide for micro-reimbursement in perpetuity, thus acknowledging the plethora of individuals who provided the original data required to design and deliver any new health product revenue stream.

Is this notion of data ownership and a web3 health future too far-flung? Or does it track with evolutionary changes that are already taking place? The latter is likely true. Let's consider a series of tailwinds that may already be propelling us forward.

HEALTH DATA IS BIG BUSINESS

Citizen health data has been fueling a mostly hidden multibillion-dollar industry for decades. It remains *mostly hidden* because patients are largely unaware of, and have not consented to, the transport of their data for these purposes.

Even with this flood of industry data, markets are desperate for real-world data. They need authenticated and aggregated diverse patient data that spans daily lifestyle routines. Clinic and hospital data is not enough to build reliable algorithms that stand the test of time, that are capable of reconstructing health.

FAVORABLE REGULATIONS ARE IN PLACE

Fortunately, a framework for regulatory oversight already exists.

The US's 21st Century Cures Act provides regulations that support more citizen agency in managing and controlling the use of health data. By the end of 2022, this rule states that individuals have the right to a computable version of their medical record. No more paper. No more PDFs. Instead, we have digital records readable by products and services supporting individual preferences.

As more businesses seek international markets, the wider regulatory framework is providing defined protections for consumers. The General Data Protection Regulation (GDPR) sets guidelines for the collection and processing of personal information from people living in the European Union.

Likewise, California has instituted their version of data protection via the California Consumer Privacy Act (CCPA), which came into effect on January 1, 2020. Meanwhile, other states are following with versions of their own.[63]

With basically nine out of every ten Americans using the internet, it is impossible for web-based products and services to meet differing sets of regulations.[64] In order to meet requirements for broad market adoption, most businesses are required to comply with the strongest set of regulations and hope that this strategy will cover them for all other versions and varieties of regulations.

COVID-19 HAS CHANGED US

However reluctantly, we have entered the domain of personal health management. For the first time, citizens have been required to have on their person verified health credentials that enable airline travel and other common public behaviors. These new behaviors may be an effective on-ramp to greater personal control over our health information.

For all the harm and deep suffering that COVID-19 has inflicted on the world, a few positive scraps have emerged. Almost immediately, people were asked to avoid in-person visits to healthcare if at all possible. At some institutions, telemedicine programs had been in the works for over two years, but with COVID-19, these once indefinite projects were fully launched; within a couple of weeks, providers were visiting with patients over the phone. More provider networks began offering online visits for cash, thus transacting directly with patients and thereby bypassing any payer-imposed restrictions. A more direct patient-to-provider access became possible.

Many of our traditionally analog behaviors moved to digital. We shopped online and visited with nurses, doctors, veterinarians, and more using phones. We put swabs into our noses, gathered saliva, and used home-testing kits. We managed our own COVID-19 care strategies with home devices such as pulse oximeters. Many of us who had a relatively mild course of COVID-19 managed the diagnosis, treatment, and isolation protocols entirely without visiting a healthcare facility. This at-home, digital-first model is a big step toward managing even more of our health ourselves using technology.

Yet our inability to effectively see around corners of human experience has been further highlighted with COVID-19. Two years into the pandemic, as the Omicron variant swept across the nation with an explosion of data, we still had little ability to predict our range of vulnerability at any time.[65] Who would be immune? How long might immunity last? Even with millions of individual vaccinations and infections, predicting vulnerability proved problematic.

Decades of encounter data covering fifteen-minute clinic visits plus intermittent hospitalizations full of medical imaging and prescription medications did little to uncover our relative risk when faced with COVID-19 infections. High-yield information, the kind that would help sort out which pockets of individuals were at higher risk and why, remained insufficient. How did the social determinants of health impact outcomes? Did living at altitude help? Did a hyper-sanitized childhood matter? Answers to these questions are not available in most medical records because high-yield elements are missing.

Another small nudge came in the form of COVID-19 reporting. For the first time, we needed to know our health status—vaccinated or not—most recent test results, and other information in order to board a plane, enter a sports facility, or just go to school, in some places. Prior to COVID-19, test results and health status would be stuck inside patient portals. We didn't typically carry or control our health data on our phones. Times are changing.

More personally controlled data options are emerging. A good example is the digital driver's license (DDL) using REAL ID. A person can obtain a DDL by scanning their physical license, taking a selfie, and completing a series of facial and head movements. Once completed, the DDL can be used for most of the typical uses we pull our driver's license out for. Perhaps we're purchasing age-restricted items, such as alcohol. The establishment need only be aware of three things: you have valid ID, you are the owner of said ID, and you meet legal age requirements. The establishment can simply use their DDL reader to scan your phone's QR code and verify all three. In this model, none of the non-required information needs to be provided. Your full name, address, license number, and more remain completely hidden.

Early in COVID-19, touching materials that might be contaminated with viruses was a concern. Some establishments stopped accepting cash. Transportation Security Administration (TSA) agents would no longer touch our phones. This further nudged states to move to using DDL and other technology that put the management of personal information in the hands of the individual.

Going through the airport for a domestic flight, the DDL informs its owner regarding the attributes requested by TSA. Unlike the bar example above, the TSA-required list is rather long: full name, date of birth, sex, ID number, state, driver's license issue and expiry date, REAL ID status, and ID photo. Apple uses built-in Face ID or Touch ID to ensure only the person who added the driver's license to the device can actually present it to anyone. To the user, it feels just like scanning a boarding pass. The individual is not required to unlock, show, or hand over their device to a TSA agent. Simply present the QR code to the reader and verification is processed.

Personally controlling our information for specific purposes is a key component of an ownership economy. Although the DDL and REAL ID efforts rely on largely web2 infrastructure, they are paving the way to a more personally controlled tomorrow.

In the meantime, there remain a few rough patches to iron out. Here the ACLU and others have raised valid concerns.[66] Could states use the DDL to gather information and track an individual's movements? Clearly if our DDL pinged or "called home" with our location each time we pulled out our DDL, that would be problematic. The state would be alerted each time we visited a bar, sports facility, medical clinic, airport, and more.

For these reasons and more, advancing this model with more web3-native technologies and leveraging blockchain and ZKPs are necessary requirements to ensure we retain the freedom to live without unauthorized data streaming to a state government or other unintended agents.

AI AND MACHINE LEARNING NEED WEB3

Support for rebalancing our current state of data power asymmetry may arrive from unpredictable sources. Clearly the use of machine learning and AI will continue to expand as more and more skills are developed in uncovering scientific truths using these tools. This may be an unexpected tailwind supporting an ownership economy. Perhaps the algorithms themselves will force a data revolution as they advance to reveal that new and robust data is required to avoid bias and unreliable outcomes. Medical encounter data is not enough.

The AI tools we know today take in large amounts of data in order to find patterns that would suggest a future outcome of interest. It's important to track patterns that occur prior to a turn for the worst in order to detect changes as early as possible. In this way, we won't miss out on corrective actions.

Often, the process for scanning data, assigning weighting, and determining whether a pattern exists or not takes place inside a *black box*. The math inside the box can be so complicated it is unexplainable even by the people who designed the algorithm.

That said, AI in healthcare is already proving to be useful for specific purposes.[67] For example, in clinical trials, about 30 percent of patients are likely to drop out of a trial.[68] This is very expensive and threatens the ability of trial sites to reach their patient targets for a particular study. Teams could design questions for trial participants that help detect those who might be on the verge of dropping out. The AI would score the answers and alert the team to potential dropouts in advance. This would trigger more attention, hand-holding, and other incentives to be advanced to these participants and safeguard against undesirable outcomes.

Clearly, protecting against study trial dropout is not a medical evaluation. Using AI and machine learning for medical insights is much less straightforward. For instance, today, experts are often disappointed with results of deep learning models using health records. Deep learning is a specialized form of machine learning that carries great promise, but sadly, resulting insights may have limited usefulness. Furthermore, it is often difficult to guard against counterintuitive and harmful recommendations that are the result of deep learning.

Brian Kihoon Lee, a research engineer and tech lead at Google Brain, has gone so far as to suggest that deep learning on electronic medical data is "doomed to fail."[69] Lee confirms that spurious correlations can be rampant and provides some telling examples. For starters, people with asthma and pneumonia seem to have better outcomes than those with pneumonia alone. Why? Well, asthma is a known risk factor for the deterioration of pneumonia. Therefore, these patients may receive higher-level intensive care more quickly—hence the correlation. The bottom line is that combining asthma with pneumonia is associated with higher severity of disease, yet the correlation suggests that people with asthma plus pneumonia are better off than those with pneumonia alone. Crazy.

In another example, machine learning models suggest that Pap tests are correlated with less heart failure. Clearly Pap tests do nothing for heart health. They are simply a marker of age. Younger people get Pap tests. Older people suffer heart failure. Lee admits that these examples are relatively easy to sort out. To be sure, as we continue to lean into AI and machine learning, especially for scientific and health-related insight, we need to be confident that any system we rely on can detect and flag spurious outcomes, no matter how sophisticated.

The bottom line is that AI, ML, and deep learning all need better data, plus continuous access to human-specific ground truths, to expose errors and course-correct. Reliable AI depends on a robust web3 version of the three-zone model outlined above.

CHAPTER NINE

WEB3 TECH IS MATURING

Web3 technology has been in development for more than a decade. Unlike the internet of information exchange (web1), web3 and blockchain provide society with an internet of trusted value exchange. Value flows in and out of complex transactions ubiquitously, and bit by bit, those especially suited to web3 tech are transforming in remarkable ways.

Take logistics and supply chain management to start. These systems have seen dramatic improvements after using distributed ledgers. Walmart Canada, for example, uses over seventy third-party freight carriers to deliver goods.[70] Invoicing for these transport services was difficult. At any time, most of the invoices required costly reconciliation efforts. Why did the invoice show eight hours for a typical four-hour commute? The questions were endless. After converting to a blockchain-like solution, the percentage of invoices under dispute dropped from 70 percent to only 2 percent.

Smart contracts and NFTs are also nothing new and are becoming more and more widely accepted. The first NFT was created in 2014 as a way of proving ownership of a digital asset. Recently, interest in NFTs has increased.

A fascinating example involves a one-hundred-year-old tax system: Australia has leveraged blockchain and NFTs to close their alcohol tax gap—taxes owed but not received. This effort, led by the Convergence.Tech team, has reported more than $45 million recovered within the first year of operation. Many millions more are expected as the project expands.

Beyond enterprises, individuals are also taking advantage of NFTs. Musicians and artists are using web3 tools to manage their assets and engage their audiences in new ways. Mixed within this new behavior are valuable learnings. What assets do people value? How can value be best tracked? How can new layers of value be added, using more and newer digitally native tools?

GAMING: A PATH TO DIGITALLY NATIVE ASSET VALUE MANAGEMENT

Another tailwind exists in the gaming industry. Granted, *game* and *gaming* may be unfortunate word choices. They suggest something unnecessary, an accessory, something that happens in the periphery of real life and takes place in one's spare time, without impact...it's "just a game." The words fail to project qualities related to being fundamental, critical, or central to creating and leveraging high-definition human knowledge, not to mention being core to new wealth creation. While we may not change the words anytime soon, I believe that we will mature our understanding of them.

What does gaming have to do with healthcare? It is no secret that healthcare understands that patients have a lot of control over most health outcomes. When outcomes are underperforming, it can be convenient to blame patients for poor adherence to recommendations. This falls under the blanket excuse of non-compliance or poor patient engagement...a continuous and real threat to optimizing population health. Figuring out health engagement is no small ask.

Consider the basics: nutrition and movement. Although many ailments would benefit from lifestyle management, practitioners have no confidence that patients will adhere to diet and exercise for any length of time. No one wakes up in the morning thinking, *I can't wait to get going on my diet and exercise.* However, increasingly large numbers of individuals do wake up energized and anxious to get going with a game on their phone. Wild. This is more than simple engagement; it might reach the criteria associated with addiction.

If healthcare could tap into an inch of the success gaming has, we might be able to engage patients sustainably in healthy behaviors.

Why does gaming work? For starters, follow the money. Using web3 tools and enabling an ownership economy within games, people are creating and purchasing digital assets online that have successfully provided passive income. Take Axie Infinity, for example, where users join a blockchain game and play to earn vital economic assets.

Citizens in the Philippines suffered catastrophic financial losses during COVID-19. Already eking out a meager existence on the smallest of incomes, this group could not afford months and years without any income. A few found their way to Axie Infinity.

Axie Infinity leverages blockchain, tokens, and NFTs. Players are required to buy three Axies that look like adorable monsters. With these, they can then breed their Axies to gain more monsters, launch them into battles, and design body parts that have special skills.

With time and attention, players in the game learn which traits and strategies are highly desirable. Savvy players soon generate Axies most capable of executing the most effective strategies that are sure to win battles. Powerful. The revolutionary part of this scenario is that any digital assets generated within the game completely belong to the player who generated them. Full stop.

Unlike other video games, where all assets belong to the hosting platform, in Axie Infinity, players can put up their Axies for sale, cash out, and buy food, pay rent, and so on in our physical world. This is not a theory.

The Filipino players scraped together the funds needed to purchase their first three Axies and went to work, literally. The game made it possible for these players to design irresistible digital assets, earn tokens in-game, sell these tokens for cryptocurrencies, and then convert these to pesos to buy food or pay rent.

The game made it possible for overseas excess currency (money available to be spent in games) to find its way into the online wallets of the poorest people without enough to survive. The rules of the game have been set by the founding team at Axie Infinity, and over time, the founders plan to convert to a DAO. This move would further the technology in the direction of a true owner economy, as central governance would be replaced with community-owned governance.

Is a play-to-earn revolution at hand? It may sound like a gimmick, but in the Philippines at least, this player-owned economy was literally a lifeline for many—a means of survival where few options previously existed.[71]

Gaming is teaching us a lot about human behavior. Who would have known that folks with extra cash would want to purchase adorable online monsters, body parts, and other in-game digital assets? Blockchain and tokens are making it easy to track who has ownership over assets on a play-by-play basis. No value can be faked, lost, or stolen. Value transfer is peer to peer, instant, and inexpensive.

Gaming provides a petri dish of sorts to better understand how some groups will behave some of the time within a low-risk environment. In healthcare, we need to be able to test out health behavior strategies within low-risk environments, such as online games. The insights learned here first would help protect against unintended consequences that might occur within a physical health setting.

Axie Infinity is an early play-to-earn video game. Videos are two-dimensional, so many will soon move to a more immersive experience using headsets and other devices that deliver virtual reality. With VR, we have the benefit of three-dimensional metaverses, and with greater immersive exchanges, the possibilities of value generation and transaction will explode yet again. Players will likely purchase land, buildings, and furniture as they move from designing cute Axies to designing their personal fortresses and vehicles for traveling between digitally exotic lands hosting limitless entertainment yet to be discovered. There will be much to unpack here.

Just as tokens track value creation and transfer, they also act as built-in incentives. Players who are playing to earn will continue to play as long as the incentives make it worth their while. Learning how to construct incentives to create desirable behaviors in virtual games may teach us how to construct better incentives to optimize human health behaviors. Can healthy habits become slightly more addictive when matching cohorts to preferred game strategies?

For many, the value proposition that we should track our steps because it is good for our health is not enough to sustain this health behavior for any length of time. Add the option to use step counts to augment our cholesterol lab data and drive the economic value of this data combination inside various marketplaces, and the value proposition takes on more meaning. Leveraging blockchain, tokens, NFTs, and federated learning, we can mix and match sophisticated value propositions that engage populations in sustainable ways. AI will be an important contributor to sorting out what works and what doesn't for diverse groups.

WEB3 OWNERSHIP ECONOMIES ARE ALREADY HAPPENING

Jesse Walden, the co-founder of an early blockchain startup which was acquired by Spotify, wrote about business empowerment through data in web2 platforms.[72] Sadly, these platforms evolve and deteriorate from cooperative to extractive practices over time.

Unlike web2, web3 enables stakeholder capitalism. In a recent post, the World Economic Forum confirms that this form of capitalism offers benefits beyond shareholder capitalism and state capitalism, and is widely seen as the basis for a global economy that works for progress, people, and the planet.[73]

Wired explained web3 as "a decentralized online ecosystem based on the blockchain. Platforms and apps built on web3 won't be owned by a central gatekeeper, but rather by users, who will earn their ownership stake by helping to develop and maintain common assets, services and marketplaces."[74]

Where is the transition from web2 to web3 most apparent? Certainly on the heels of the 2008 recession, a new set of digital rails appeared without impacting much, if any, of the traditional financial establishment at the time. After more than a decade, the bitcoin blockchain operating outside of and separate to commonly used banking infrastructure continues to provide value to an increasing number of users. This is the only example of a truly distributed network enabling stakeholder capitalism—ownership, potentially for eight billion people.

The bitcoin blockchain is an organic entity growing from the contributions of people. No one is home in terms of a central management team. Perhaps unnoticed by most, distributed networks in healthcare are also already forming.

THE CANNABIS INDUSTRY LEADING THE WAY FORWARD

The use of cannabis as a household therapeutic for sleep, pain, anxiety, and other ailments happens largely outside of traditional medicine, just as the bitcoin blockchain operates outside of traditional financial rails. Participants use web3 tech to deliver early forms of stakeholder capitalism to their communities, which improves the finances of industry business models and ensures therapeutic benefit is delivered in experience-based ways.

Let's consider two key differentiators: a new framework for debt financing—an *open* credit model that assigns risk while protecting business trade secrets—and crowdsourced experience-based intelligence using the privacy and security of web3 tools.

A NEW FRAMEWORK FOR DEBT FINANCING

In 2018, the Small Business Administration (SBA) blocked banks from lending to or banking with the cannabis industry. This move meant that teams would have to scale their business using only equity capital and not a preferred balance of equity and debt capital as in other industries. The preferred corporate debt-to-equity ratio is typically 4:3, but with the SBA ruling, equity capital swelled to five times the debt capital in cannabis.

Both banks and private capital are sources of debt, but with banks out, why has private capital not expanded more? Debt in a market reflects the aggregate risk of loan failure, but not in the cannabis industry. Lack of public debt access also blocks standard risk ranking mechanisms (such as those used by the three main credit rating agencies, S&P Global Ratings [S&P], Moody's, and Fitch Group), and there is no loss protection guarantee with private loans.

Enter Chroma Signet, a web3 product delivering credit risk analysis and supporting debt capital transactions in the cannabis industry. This product solves two main problems: the cost of collecting corporate/business-relevant data and the risk of sharing this data.

Chroma Signet uses network finance to support debt capital. While banks typically see businesses as an island, network finance assesses the creditworthiness of the supply chain and assesses risk of the branch (business) in a network. It looks at both the borrower and their supply chain creditworthiness, exposing both the upstream and downstream credit conditions to generate a full financial risk assessment.

How does this help? Factoring is usually seller-led, with the seller offering a discount to the buyer for rapid pay. Chroma Signet enables reverse factoring: a buyer-led transaction where a financier agrees to pay the seller's invoice at an accelerated rate in exchange for a discount to avoid a thirty- to ninety-day delay. In this way, suppliers will accept a 95 percent payment via Chroma Signet, with the extra 5 percent showing up on the lender's balance sheet once the full loan is paid.

The financial risk assessment algorithm is open for public inspection and improvement, while the specific identities of suppliers and customers remain cryptographically hidden. In this way, the industry can offer up improvements to the algorithm while not gaining access to the business secrets of competitors, such as the identity of various suppliers and customers.

Since governments have mandated seed-to-sale data in this industry, Chroma Signet makes collecting the data easy with little need to normalize. The supply chain data, seed to sale, is valuable input to credit models but must be protected from inappropriate sharing with other parties. Chroma Signet uses zk-SNARK, a zero-knowledge succinct non interactive argument of knowledge encryption. Thus, companies can submit private data to the credit model without risk of follow-on use of private content.

This approach flips the model of national credit agents such as S&P, Moody's, and Fitch Group, which were large participants in the financial crisis of 2008. The black box approach to algorithms can result in generating substantially more risk than expected. Without access to the assessment strategy, investors have little way of determining when opportunity risk exceeds their comfort level.

This point bears repeating; unlike our national credit assessment agents, Chroma Signet hides the data but keeps the credit models that consume data and assign risk open for ongoing assessment and improvement. As more and more businesses depend upon the power of networks, using this *open* credit assessment model is likely to become commonplace.

CROWDSOURCED EXPERIENCE-BASED INTELLIGENCE

It may sound aspirational that the experiences of scores of individuals could be safely connected in such a way that no experience goes to waste, but managing a flood of moving parts and identifying potentially relevant co-occurrences is simple work for machine-based artificial intelligence. No longer do the yoga routines that protect against migraines simply evaporate; instead, these experiences are collected and digitized, thus making them safely explorable among the thousands of other co-occurrences that might matter. With web3 approaches, the human health experience of many can collaborate to inform groups and individuals regarding the benefits or lack thereof of certain therapeutic options.

CBD, or cannabidiol, compounds are the portions of marajuana that contain no mind-altering effects but have been found to be helpful for a number of health conditions. Thus, CBD has become an active component of various products. These, however, do not fit within traditional therapeutics, and as such, securing funding for large, rigorous randomized controlled trials remains problematic. Natural products are difficult to patent, and without a route to intellectual property rights, reliable business models leading to hefty profits are much less likely. There must be another way.

Teasing out what works for which symptoms in which individuals is not an easy task. There is likely to be significant variation in personal response to various plant products over time. Interestingly, gender differences in responses have been reported.

CLOSING THE LOOP = WHAT IS IT? + HOW WELL DOES IT WORK?

A seed-to-sale value chain that also includes therapeutic utility across diverse cohorts over time relies on a stakeholder capitalism support system. Smart Cannabis, for instance, is a software service that collects and analyzes customer experiences so that products and their effects can be reliably connected. Private, secure, and certifiable customer experiences remain the driving force for successful business growth in the cannabis market, and as such, customers are rewarded for sharing their experiences with tokens and cash-back options.

Corrin has difficulty sleeping due to chronic back pain. He's used opioids and sedatives in the past but finds the withdrawal difficult. His online support group suggested he try a specific combination product. It took several nights before Corrin was convinced this new product was helping. He uploaded his experience daily to keep track of his own progress and hopefully help others who might be struggling with similar pain. Now, eight months later, Corrin continues to find benefit from this and other recommended natural products. He is hopeful that opioids and prescription sedatives will be a rare and last resort for outlier episodes of breakthrough pain.

Imagine Corrin uses his SSI to log into his Smart Cannabis app and scans the barcode of the product he uses. This provides a genetic mapping of the product, a complete list of ingredients, with seed-to-sale provenance data. He then adds his before-and-after symptom data and possible aggravating or alleviating factors with his dose and timing data. The platform rewards Corrin with tokens and discounts for future purchases. In this way, Corrin can track his specific use of natural products for his own benefit while contributing to the experience-based evidence pool that benefits all participants.

This cooperative stakeholder capitalism model ensures that businesses have dynamic real-world access to what is working at the level of the consumer. By using federated learning approaches, the specifics of Corrin's experience can remain on his own devices while analytic tools access preapproved portions of data to feed algorithms searching for clinically relevant correlations. In this way, businesses uncover what works, which products may be superior to others, and which products may be redundant or missing from their offering. Technology provides detailed, blinded, and unbiased research to businesses seeking to detect which products perform well while uncovering new customer segments that are more likely to expand their market.

Individual biology is unfathomably complex. Using machines alone to simulate this complexity remains problematic. Furthermore, people have buying power; machines do not. Populating the planet with people brimming with vigorous health and robust buying power supports all economies. With web3 we can leverage new ways of collaborating with built-in privacy-protecting elements while reaping the business benefits.

As customers deliberately support businesses by privately sharing their experiences, they are ensuring industry continues to advance in a safe and evidence-based manner. Over time, therapeutic recommendations will become increasingly personalized as each individual benefits from those that went before.

Web3-supported stakeholder capitalism provides a path to unprecedented, reliable intelligence and, in turn, greater wealth co-creation. People who contribute to *answers*, as well as the answers themselves, can then be tokenized and sold within Zone III. This commercial zone would have access to permissioned real-world experience-based evidence as outlined in the previous cannabis example. Unprecedented access to ground truths will lead to new combination therapies, unlock new markets, and co-create new wealth.

Meanwhile, within Zone I, people can put their personal fiduciary AI to use answering requests for information or auto-approving transactions based on their preset selections. Perhaps Matt's requirements before sharing personal data include a minimum payment offer of fifty dollars per request, the requester must be within his country, and the requester must have disclosed a purpose or goal that meets one of his stated defaults. Built-in smart contracts, native to various blockchain systems, will likely manage the bulk of these requests for authorization.

We live at a time when widespread automation is impacting the global employment landscape. Just as we use doctors and lawyers to navigate complicated sectors of our lives, digital fiduciaries are likely to be indispensable to a safe and secure navigation of ever-changing digital environments. Still, there remains much to sort out.

For starters: Who owns the data? The clinic, the hospital, the payer, or the person? Do we settle on ownership or instead discuss rights similar to water rights? To what degree will the multibillion-dollar medical-industrial complex continue to dig in its heels with respect to citizen-centric data practices?

At least initially, large stakeholders may not be convinced that permissioned data is likely to carry more value than current approaches. Perhaps avoidance of massive ransom attacks and data breaches will be enough to entice the dominant players to shift toward person-centric approaches. Gone would be the honeypots of data; these represent a single attack surface, which is ideal for those seeking to break into the data. One successful breach can result in unauthorized access to the entire data set. Replace this with a highly distributed storage model, and suddenly there are thousands of tiny data islands rendering efforts to steal data impractical. Too much effort for such little gain.

What is clear at this point is that people increasingly want and deserve agency over their personal data. Many expect data management policies to require expressed approval and include the patient in any follow-on compensation.[75] Perhaps it will simply be inevitable that a mass citizen migration takes place. People will inevitably choose citizen-oriented provider networks that make it easy to carry and control our personal records while engaging in marketplaces to gain passive income. NFTs and federated learning are likely to play a significant role in providing this personal agency over our digital assets.

Over time, we expect correlations from Zone II will drive a plethora of ground truth intelligence that underpins innovation in the products and services generated in Zone III. But who will pay for this? We have learned in our current web2 era that hosting data can be expensive, cumbersome, and risky. If the patients are indeed hosting and managing their own data such that high-quality information is available at every health encounter, this would be a massive cost savings for health delivery networks. Would it be enough of a cost savings that health systems would pay patients to host their own data? Would health systems compete for out-of-network customers by financially supporting personal health records? Would vulnerable populations have up-to-date records that could avoid repeating a series of tests that have already been performed? Scratching the economics out on the back of a napkin will not suffice.

What does this mean for our current web2 healthcare ecosystem? Surely healthcare will continue to manage the heavyweight decisions: the right drug or procedure for the right person at the right time; surgery; emergency care. The difference is, as citizens—with the help of AI—we will take on more ownership of our mundane personal health needs, and in turn, doctors, medical establishments, and hospital systems will find themselves more empowered to lead in the places where they have traditionally been strongest.

Still, even with the tailwinds highlighted above, pushback is inevitable. In Part V, let's explore some of the arguments *against* the type of web3 healthcare this book proposes and share a number of counterarguments in support of our preferred future.

PART V

PUSHING THROUGH PUSHBACK

CHAPTER TEN

PUSHBACK IS INEVITABLE

Our biology is suffering at the hands of advancing technology, yet to reverse the status quo, we must actually use technology in order to provide our biology a reliable voice to speak truth to power. Though occasionally perplexing, there remains common garden-variety pushback today. Proponents of a web3 health solution would benefit from addressing these head-on.

Can we truly provide a safe means by which the many can co-produce biological truths while preserving personal privacy? How will technology become a continuously evolving protective force that ensures we all have access to our optimal health futures in time to make a difference? How would technology deliver these truths, along with a multitude of potential roadmaps, such that we might choose our life directions on our own terms?

Part III conceptualized a technology architecture that could very well deliver the type of crowdsourced biological truths we currently lack. Part IV discussed a number of ways in which this new reality is already taking shape. However, plenty of questions and uncertainties remain. Are we capable of killing the golden goose before it lays a golden egg?

If a web3 health infrastructure would be truly transformational, why hasn't it happened already? Core technologies have been around for years. As I shared in Part IV, plenty of traction points in this direction. The finance sector has invested handsomely in digital cash, as well as the infrastructure to support more complex derivatives and other financial products. Gaming is using blockchain and NFTs to manage in-game assets, and their audience is growing—and seems addicted to participating.

So if a web3 ownership economy, based on Part III's three-zone approach, really has the potential to create both health and wealth, wouldn't it have happened already? Actually, no. There are a few reasons why this will take time.

THE TECH IS NOT READY

As of right now, the technology is too expensive, potentially environmentally destructive, and too complicated for retail users. The speed and expense issues impair the opportunity to scale the solutions. As the number of transactions expands from thousands, to hundreds of thousands, to millions, the core infrastructure becomes problematic.

With blockchain, every node on the system has to verify every transaction. This means we're limited to what a single computer can hold. By adding a second layer, aptly called layer two, on top, you can shrink the number of nodes (as in the number of computers) that need to verify most transactions and only "check in" with the expensive and slow layer one–or base blockchain–intermittently.

Take Ethereum, for instance. The base chain can manage fifteen transactions per second; add a layer two and one thousand to five thousand transactions are possible. Add to this sharding (database partitioning such that transactions can move to smaller, faster, and more easily managed mechanisms) or roll-ups (batching transactions onto modular blockchains that need only *check-in* intermittently with the parent blockchain) and the transaction rate skyrockets to one hundred thousand transactions per second. Transactions that were once very expensive and slow can leverage new methods to become exceedingly quick and low cost at the same time.

DIGITALLY NATIVE SOLUTIONS ARE TOO VOLATILE

Volatility is associated with innovation. Recall that when the dotcom bubble burst, some predicted the end of the World Wide Web. Clearly that didn't happen. What happened instead was a type of cleaning house. Companies providing real value survived, while others failed. Nothing new.

Frequent ups and downs have been associated with digitally native crypto assets since their inception. Occasionally, however, massive movements take place. During the writing of this book, we moved firmly from a mostly bull market to a broad bear market. Product launches decreased, trading volumes dropped, and retail engagement plummeted, resulting in most assets dropping by 50 percent or more. Does this spell the end of crypto or web3?

No. We've seen this before. New technology is hard to get right. A lot of experiments are launched. Hopefully we learn from most of them. Those that tank when the bubble bursts tend to hold the least value for the community, while others weather the storm and emerge stronger than before. Opinions vary. Perhaps Bitcoin and Ethereum are more solid contenders for recession-proof status, while others make up a long tail of experiments. Jolts to the ecosystem help sort which projects matter most. Life is not a straight line. Technology is no different.

THE ENVIRONMENTAL IMPACT IS TOO MUCH

A common misconception is that Bitcoin mining is bad for the environment. Very bad.

To be clear, *mining* here refers to the mechanism used by thousands of specialized computers to solve computationally complex puzzles. Scores of miners (people owning these specialized computers) work to secure the bitcoin blockchain. They are participating in an effort known as a consensus mechanism called proof-of-work (PoW). This PoW consensus mechanism confirms transactions and maintains the trustworthiness of the blockchain. Miners are incentivized to complete these puzzles as the winner (the first to solve it) is rewarded with Bitcoin—a hefty sum.

Back to the environment. Running these specialized computers (mining machines) utilizes a lot of energy—so much so that the Chinese government actually banned all mining in China. This resulted in a glut of mining machines available for purchase and followed with a mining boom in the US. This might not be all bad. Nic Carter explains that mining is America's most misunderstood industry.

Miners have learned how to take advantage of their unique attributes. Firstly, they can locate themselves anywhere there is a connection to the internet. So, for obvious reasons, they will seek out stranded excess energy sources that are likely to be more inexpensive. Another unique attribute is that miners can withstand power interruptions without significantly impairing their operations. This makes them the ideal customer for power grids heavy with renewables, such as wind and sun.

Energy grids are a continuous balancing act. Troy Cross, a fellow at the Bitcoin Policy Institute, explains that mining is the best demand-side customer. Mining takes surplus loads and converts them into money. With renewables, the ebb and flow of surplus wind or sun is difficult to control. Miners are good at scooping up stranded excess power and rescuing the economics of wind and solar installations that might otherwise be lost without the helping hand of an on-demand heavy consumer, such as Bitcoin mining.

As much as two-thirds of electricity can be lost to curtailment, which is the deliberate reduction in available energy to balance transmission restraints. Simply turning down the "on" switch creates a loss of potentially useful energy. In short, green or renewable energy is good for the planet, but not good for the grid. Crypto mining has been called a dung beetle of surplus energy–it can seek out overlooked sources and soak them up, turning energy into cash. For more details about mining, check out the writings of Dennis Porter, the CEO and co-founder of the Satoshi Action Fund.

As we decarbonize our economy, more and more electricity will predominate, and we will need more mining machines to soak up any surplus energy and ensure the grid remains balanced.

Note: the older mining machines are best suited to realize this vision as they tolerate significant swings in uptime. Newer mining rigs are less flexible and might be less well suited.

Finally, here's another perspective we might consider: take a moment to compare energy consumption of these consensus mechanisms to the energy and carbon footprint of mega skyscraper industries, such as banking, escrow, and clearinghouses. Energy costs of these brick-and-mortar companies include heat, lighting, maintenance, and upgrades, not to mention employees that drive to and from work most days of the week. Assuming a shift away from physical spaces to more online peer-to-peer digital transactions with wallets and a metaverse, perhaps the drop in carbon footprint from our physical world would balance most of the new and added carbon footprint of the digital replacements for our physical worlds.

WEB3 AND DAOS ARE NOT MAGIC

The term *web3* is simply shorthand, technical slang, and jargon. It implies the next iteration of the internet—a quick way to reference a sentiment and ethos supporting ownership or stakeholder economies. Also implied within web3 are the technical underpinnings, including blockchain, crypto, tokens, and other tools designed to reliably deliver this next internet iteration for society.

Shorthand, however, can be problematic if, in service of brevity, web3 becomes misunderstood as magic, an inevitability, or a de facto solution of sorts.

No one knows if web3 will deliver us from evil or alter the asymmetry that plagues the current internet. In fact, progress is not inevitable. Tech is easy, but organizations are based on people, and people can be tricky. How do we manage obligations or rights that participants have within any form of organization?

The traditional company, complete with CEO and executive team, has organized groups around a common purpose. Sadly, even companies with problematic behaviors seem to thrive for decades. They might underpay workers, overpay shareholders, and invest heavily in lobbying to promote self-serving legislation.

In response to these issues, cooperatives have evolved over the last couple of centuries, with varying success. These seek to provide more economic opportunity for all by expanding broad-based ownership and alternative finance models. With time, these cooperatives have built robust legal wrappers. Learning from years of claims against cooperatives, a broad fact pattern emerged to inform the legal requirements for intentional expectation management. Thus important safeguards have evolved. These protect the founding team, as well as participants, against liabilities that arise from other participants or the cooperative itself.

So, do we even need DAOs? Companies, cooperatives, and now DAOs provide different governance structures to organize groups of people. They are taxonomies of the same beast. Will DAOs survive? It is too early to tell. But if adaptation is the key to survival, then DAOs fit the bill.

A DAO is an organization that is built on blockchain transparency and accountability, which also offers a bridge between being a worker and owning a portion of the value generated. DAOs are expected to be nimbler and less limited than a cooperative. They will provide reliable, fast, inexpensive, and broad participation out of the box, with an even wider design potential. More new and flexible incentive and voting models are expected to onboard participants and drive scalability beyond traditional approaches to organizing groups of individuals.

The flood of capital into DAOs will inevitably drive actions by regulators, which may be problematic. Hence, the broader DAO community is working to provide guidelines that would reduce risks for those participating in DAOs.

Joshua Tan, executive director of the Metagovernance Project, is working on modularizing a framework for complex institutional innovation. The goal is to provide newly organized groups the tools to mix and match various governance approaches that might work best for their particular needs. Ideally, a modular solution, almost like add-on Legos, would lower the barrier for trying various approaches to group governance. Tan recognizes that each new social structure is different and no single tech solution will magically work for everyone.

In the beginning, social systems typically look very familiar. They enlist a small dedicated team with a centralized *benevolent dictator for life* (BDFL) that is responsible for the early heavy lifting. The aim, however, is to progressively decentralize to a different target state—one that is more inclusive and serves participants in a nonhierarchical way.

The Ownership Economy podcast covers an example of this governance transition model: Chobani yogurt.[76] Here, the founder became a billionaire off yogurt sales and then decided to give a majority of the equity to the people who built it. This is a rare outcome for most companies that lack a structural imperative to do so.

DAOs seek to design incentives that ensure progressive decentralization of ownership over time. The hope is that DAOs will be able to build in the Chobani model—that is, designing at the outset a set of rights that provides for ownership of future value, which is co-produced by the participants. Project tokens are used as membership access to track participants, as well as labor contributions, to the DAO.

A simple governance model is the *one token equals one vote* model. However, when tokens can be purchased and used to control governance, those with the means to purchase more likely control more voting rights and the project takes on centralized power asymmetries of the past. More thoughtful token economics are needed to build and sustain progressive decentralization that works for all participants.

Nathan Schneider, scholar, activist, and journalist, reminds us that technology typically amplifies the power relationships that already exist. Without a careful design strategy, are we at risk of building a new class of monopolies with even deeper forms of centralized power? Figuring out how to combine the best of blockchain-based DAO infrastructure with worker cooperatives is already underway.

Jason Prado, director of platform at the Drivers Cooperative, has built a rideshare service that is 100 percent owned and managed by drivers. Though the mega rideshare platforms (Uber and

Lyft) likely listen to driver input, this input effort may resemble a focus group-like activity. Without question, Uber and Lyft decide at any given moment which worker has access to rides. In this model, drivers fear that they are simply one ride away from extinction. One grumpy passenger, one low-ranking review, and poof, access could be eliminated. Drivers may have little recourse. The Drivers Cooperative seeks to provide incentive models that protect drivers and passengers in new ways.

Can healthcare learn from these new forms of organization? Complex health problems require input from diverse expertise as well as large patient populations. Could DAOs be the path to faster, more personally relevant solutions?

Imagine a group of patients decide to form a Long COVID-19 DAO. A group of like-minded individuals with a strong conviction to act meet via social media. They set up a small leadership team, and then the heavy lifting starts: holding meetings, engaging in community building, organizing notes, creating content, recruiting experts, defining labor needs, and more. This activity is typically volunteer work; without a shared financial resource, the group does not benefit from setting up a DAO yet.

Once momentum builds, the next step is to generate a white paper that will lay the groundwork for attracting funding—a shared financial resource. The white paper provides Long COVID-19 background information, knowledge gaps, and a project plan to fill these gaps and generate new value in the form of detailed specifications for future health products and services. With help from the Metagovernance Project, the team selects governance modules and defines the Long COVID-19 DAO (LCD) token economics: how many tokens will be minted, what number goes to the team, and how others can purchase tokens, provide labor or data, or otherwise participate in the Long COVID-19 DAO.

LCD tokens provide for new incentives, but incentives can be tricky. Tracking value can be difficult, and determining how valuable any contribution might be in the future is difficult. You might remember that Justin Rosenstein invented the *Like* button, originally on Facebook and now used across many social media platforms. It might have seemed a trivial contribution at the start, but it clearly went on to generate outsized revenue for Facebook. It remains unclear whether Rosenstein gained any financial benefit from a simple *Like* button that went on to extreme success.

Healthcare's Rosenstein might be Lacks. In 1951, Henrietta Lacks visited her doctor, who took cells from her cervix and diagnosed her with cancer. Unknown to her or her physician, these cells went on to become immortal—they successfully procreated and soon formed the basis of countless more cell cultures. These cell cultures could be edited for various scientific inquiry and have led to a multitude of discoveries decades beyond the quiet passing of Henrietta, the cell "donor." Henrietta did not have an opportunity to consent to the use of her tissues beyond the original intent, nor did she or her family benefit financially from follow-on financial gains.

Would a modern-day Henrietta be able to mint a token that would lay claim to all future use cases involving her cell line? Perhaps not yet. Health DAOs protecting Long COVID-19 participants in new ways may be more near-term. However, participating in these DAOs assumes that we all benefit from a common IT infrastructure that is protected as a human right. Adrian Gropper, the CTO of Patient Privacy Rights, suggests that personal information infrastructure must be treated in the same way we treat infrastructure for clean water—as a fundamental human right.[77]

Motivated patient community DAOs can mint tokens and specify under which conditions they would be available to individual members. Purchasing LCD using fiat (government-issued currency, such as the US dollar), sharing data, answering questionnaires, inviting or recruiting participants, providing patient narratives, and more could be rewarded in tokens.

Will these tokens be regulated as security tokens? Will they be utility tokens? Perhaps DAOs that can demonstrate effective decentralization will be able to avoid unfavorable regulation.

There remains much to work out. What is the exit plan? Will DAO participants be able to take their tokens and jump ship to another, more preferred, DAO? Will members be able to simply leave on demand? How would we *take our toys and go home*?

At this point, the motivation for DAOs is real. Elon Musk proved that making a better model would indeed result in mass migration from gas-powered to electric vehicles. Is the DAO the Tesla of organizations? Will mass migration to worker-owned economies be inevitable? Are the days of private platforms numbered? Is the metaverse to be the equivalent of the town commons?

Highly regarded experts are spending hours on building blocks, and yet Tan reminds us of the possibility of a DAO dystopia: a world in which true believers hop onto a tech stack that builds an oligarchy.[78] All the work value goes directly to a small set of people, and web3 winds up looking a lot like web2.

This fear is all too real. Consider the following:

When open-source software, or OSS (computer language/code that is widely available for use, modification, and distribution by other developers), first came on the scene, many were shocked. Free and open software would never compete with the enterprise-grade software that came with a heavy price tag. Soon, however, it was clear that OSS was more reliable, more economical, and easier to maintain. *With many eyes, all bugs are shallow.* Building software with crowds of developers was infinitely better than building it with just a few.

Some eighty three million software developers contribute to the open-source community on GitHub. Together they commit code, track bugs, and fix features. Microsoft, a private and for-profit company, supported this community for over a decade. All was good. Developers dumped packages of free OSS onto the GitHub platform. Then, without a lot of fanfare, a commercial, for-profit product called Copilot was announced.

What? Clearly most of the eighty three million developers had not anticipated such a move. There is no easy way of *picking up your code and going home.* Follow-on value is even more complicated to correct at this juncture, since AI-assisted writing of code is commonplace. The early, free OSS, generously supplied by developers, is likely largely responsible for AI-assisted tools in the first place. Follow-on AI-generated code will self-train without the need for humans in the loop. Thus, AI, once dependent upon the OSS coded by developers, becomes immortal in a sense. The AI becomes autonomous and royalties funnel to a few. Who would have dreamed that a bastion of free and open productivity could turn on a dime? Perhaps the collective value generated over the decade was too great to resist. Hoping for good capital behavior may be unrealistic, and of course, hope is not a strategy.

Crowdsourced value in software and crowdsourced health intelligence share attributes.

With OSS, humans collaborate in generative value production that is non-rivalrous. Similarly, physicians and medical intelligence generally have long relied on open education and generative knowledge. Morbidity and mortality rounds highlight, in full color, what went wrong, in the hopes of avoiding any repeats and advancing medical knowledge for everyone.

As soon as you move to the Copilot model, separate efforts stop learning from each other. Algorithms become black box intellectual property. This means separate device companies will likely have similar bugs that generate similar harms as they fail to inform each other of any bugs already identified. AI may be a tiny fraction of health operations today, but expect this to become a majority in a few short years. Is there another way?

Could eighty three million developers be part of a DAO? Will we utilize off-the-shelf modules from the Metagovernance Project such that participants cannot be scammed a decade later? Will the DAO come up with new licensing arrangements that reward participants in perpetuity? Will the co-created value be self-sustaining and recursive such that DAOs truly become autonomous and fund their own existence? No humans in the loop?

This might be too much to consider at the moment. At least we're clear that a valid alternative to the Microsoft/GitHub model could be the new *Tesla* of OSS, spurring a mass migration of millions of developers.

THE TOKEN ECONOMICS OF PERSONAL HEALTH WOULD BE TOO DIFFICULT

Experiments are ongoing in gaming, finance, and many other sectors—and certainly we are moving into new territory here. Meanwhile, history reminds us of where we've been. In fact, we already know what the bookends look like.

On the one end is zero tokenization, which produced our Henrietta Lacks story: mega value created with zero ownership attributed to the individuals originating this value. On the other end of the spectrum is the fully decentralized bitcoin blockchain: here, each participant fully owns their fraction of available value (coin). Surely an effective and tokenized personal health ecosystem would land and evolve somewhere in between.

Health data markets depend on access to authentic health experiences with verifiable provenance. Does this mean I can be rewarded with tokens for sharing bits of my breast cancer journey? Yes and no. Simply "paying" for data elements with tokens could yield an unlimited volume of data contribution; thus, over time the value of each individual token would decrease. Total token numbers are best capped at a certain amount, such as hundreds of millions or a few billion. Built-in actions, such as "burning" tokens and others, help to avoid value deterioration.

Novel token mechanisms are the subject of each white paper that underpins new protocols.

Recently, Vitalik Buterin, creator of Ethereum, and others published, "Decentralized Society: Finding Web3's Soul." This paper proposes a token model that would provide a web3-native human social identity. The authors discuss an identity made up of Soulbound Tokens (SBTs) representing commitments, credentials, affiliations, and more. Others attest to these attributes, thus ensuring verifiable provenance of the credentials, and so on.[79]

We could imagine such a model supporting a personal health data marketplace. My breast cancer diagnosis could be attested to by my oncologist. Chemotherapy treatments would be attested to via the clinics, complete with time and place. In this way, the social context of my health experience would be logged in an immutable manner using blockchain.

Any imposter hoping to gain the financial lift of in-demand health data by faking a health record would be out of luck. It would be next to impossible to generate the social context of a real six months in the life of a breast cancer patient. Imagine trying to fake repeat health visits to specific practitioners and clinics over time. SBTs ensure real people and real relationships among specific health journeys can be made available to health data marketplaces.

While eliminating individual fraudulent behavior in healthcare is of great value, SBTs could also help generate communities with specific attributes. Health researchers looking for individuals that carry certain traits could use this model to detect individuals that authentically and verifiably match the traits needed. Together, the authors provide a vision of a decentralized society as "DeSoc—a co-determined sociality where souls and communities come together bottom-up, as emergent properties of each other to co-create plural network goods, including plural intelligences, at a range of social scales."[80]

Figuring out the token economics migrating within and between all three zones is beyond the scope of this effort. Thankfully, others have proposed parallel systems with keen overlap.

HEALTHCARE ISN'T BUILT TO INNOVATE

Healthcare innovation *is* extremely slow, and the industry has a long history of lagging behind transformation. Healthcare likes to dig its heels in when it comes to change. Remember when the electronic medical record was a new thing? Clearly, illegible handwritten notes in paper records sorted on wooden shelves inside of clinics and hospitals should be a thing of the past by now, especially when records sometimes go missing at precisely the time we professionals need them for a patient's visit.

At the time when digital was still a new idea, businesses everywhere began going in that direction, realizing untold efficiencies in the process. At the same time, there was no shortage of vendors hoping to land electronic medical records (EMR) contracts with major healthcare providers. Physician practices were flooded with sales folks offering to modernize health records management. Clearly we'd be right to expect a guaranteed major windfall for any investor in digital record systems. What could go wrong? Turns out, this logic was wrong.

Remarkably, there was almost no adoption. Paper records persisted. Change finally came when the US government passed a Meaningful Use program as part of the Health Information Technology for Economic and Clinical Health (HITECH) Act in 2009. These regulations forced physicians to submit bills electronically if the payer was government, the Centers for Medicare and Medicaid Services (CMS). More than 50 percent of a typical facility's billing goes to the CMS. But without an electronic bill, the practice would not be paid.

Billing was the core need. EMR systems, designed as billing solutions first and foremost, had difficulty fitting into the practitioner's workflow. Physicians to this day lament the intrusion an EMR has on the doctor-patient relationship.

Not only is our medical-industrial complex very slow, but the promise of digital records launching more aggressive leaps in health intelligence has still not materialized. The industry has remarkably rickety access to biological truths. Individuals and families suffer the consequences of unreliable health intelligence that fails to advance at the pace of change. While communities remain on standby, mostly distanced from deliberate co-production of health intelligence, evidence of faulty knowledge persists.

However, when you consider the speed at which COVID-19 tech made its way to the market, it offers a glimpse of just how quickly healthcare *can* move in times of crisis. But again, responding to crises—that is, big events—is what our traditional "sickcare" model is all about.

Three decades after a well-meaning United States Department of Agriculture (USDA) food pyramid provided nutritional guidance to Americans, we're still suffering unintended consequences. The guidance launched a low-fat craze with nutritional patterns that have persisted to this day. Long story short, experts such as David Ludwig, endocrinologist and researcher, and others suggest the USDA food pyramid's recommendations likely played a part in the subsequent surge in American obesity.[81] Our health intelligence failed to deliver health to the population. Decades later, we're still trying to course-correct and, for many individuals, the die has been cast and reversibility seems improbable, if not impossible.

Healthcare also has a laundry list of procedures that have proven harmful. Recall the massive trend of silicone breast implants, with over four hundred thousand procedures per year. Decades of patient complaints later, resolution of the negative fallout remains painfully slow. Patient registries are insufficient. Rapid access to the truth is needed to avoid unintended outcomes.

We also have a list of blockbuster drugs that have generated a problematic track record over the years. Recall Actos, also known as pioglitazone. This drug is a thiazolidinedione and is used in patients living with Type II diabetes. At one point, sales made up a full quarter of the revenue generated by the manufacturer. Many problems surfaced, including cancer, and decades later, legal and financial settlements occurred. Meanwhile, the drug remains approved for use by the FDA.

Let's not forget the environmental toxins that flow into communities without correction: lead in Flint, Michigan; radon in older homes; agricultural pesticides; and more. These problems persist for decades despite devastating family losses. Imagine a single neighborhood with four children all diagnosed with the same rare cancer. Sounds suspicious, but even then, evidence was deemed insufficient to force action.

Families need to be able to protect themselves and their communities. Biological truths can remain hidden within web2. Data power asymmetry can be deadly.

Even excellent peer-reviewed science can be problematic. We rely on it to provide the basis of human health intelligence, but science, no matter how high quality or how rigorous, is often too expensive and too slow for most of us. Furthermore, citizens often don't realize that current approaches only provide a small fraction of the truth.

Studies with positive results are publishable. If a study proves negative results (it failed to show the expected results), it will not be published. Hence, the scientific community remains largely unaware of what didn't work and why. Furthermore, the majority of published scientific studies are not reproducible.[82] This means they cannot be validated either by the same researchers or by other researchers. We need an upgraded way to produce human health intelligence.

Finally, patients often report that practitioners do not take their concerns seriously. On occasion, patients are finally diagnosed with serious illnesses only after months of visiting various clinicians. To fix this, experts suggest more training is the answer. Physicians need to learn to better remove bias and other physician-centric behaviors that might interfere with accurate diagnosis. Fix the doctor to avoid unintended consequences?

Perhaps arm the patient with comprehensive personal health narratives that can be fact-checked across hundreds of records like hers to highlight high-probability correlations. The digitally augmented doctor-patient relationship is likely to benefit from a hefty data-driven lift in accurate diagnoses.

It may seem obvious that an ownership economy would help patients provide personal and accurate data to clinicians caring for them, but another problem, perhaps less obvious, relates to mergers and acquisitions. When health systems change hands, our private details can be caught in the crosshairs.

INDUSTRY WON'T GIVE UP CONTROL OF OUR DATA

Not too long ago, the Oracle purchase of Cerner was in the news. Oracle provides software and databases aimed at optimizing many different enterprise operations. Oracle's customers span well beyond healthcare. Cerner, on the other hand, is a fully healthcare-centric record management system that contains the private details of every patient who visited a provider using the Cerner record system.

What scares me most about this is the lack of comment from our learned colleagues who have deep expertise in the patient data space. Many of us read these headlines and feel a cozy confidence that others with Ivy League degrees and the ability to articulate with profound eloquence will pipe up to lay bare the between-the-lines ramifications in no uncertain terms—but I haven't found those posts, op-eds, or long-form articles. This is indeed problematic.

Clearly Oracle is not buying just medical billing software.

Included in such a transaction would be each and every private detail of any interaction I may have had with a Cerner provider... all fully identified. Not during any of these private visits with medical providers did the possibility of my data going to Oracle ever come up.

Clearly we may extend some grace to Cerner. They built a medical data management system within the constraints of a web2 internet. Asking patients to own and manage their personal health information was completely unreasonable a few short years ago—hence the era of massive honeypots of personal health information, medical data breaches, and ransom attacks.

Oracle, on the other hand, has been a pure tech company. Without a doubt, the increasing migration of web2 to web3 infrastructures are core to their understanding of tech innovation. Could our more learned colleagues be aware of this? Are the old rumors of Oracle as a predator no longer valid? Does Oracle see a Cerner acquisition as a necessary building block to a much preferred tomorrow? One that enables healthcare to advance beyond PowerPoints suggesting patient-centric solutions to one that actually sports a tech stack that puts the patient at the center of her healthcare? Should I expect a blockchain-based longitudinal health record that I own and control to rapidly become the norm? Will I be able to engage in health data marketplaces of my own choosing? Has Oracle already posted a litany of content detailing the injustices of our current web2 architecture and the imperative to adopt web3 solutions?

I haven't found this content, which is frightening. I am desperately hoping my colleagues are about to unleash a swarm of their typically polished pieces—papers that remind us of the perils of centralized systems. When we swap out one master for an even larger master, turning the *Titanic* toward our preferred tomorrow may be that much more difficult.

AI AND ML STRUGGLE AGAINST HARMFUL RECOMMENDATIONS

IBM Watson is a question-answering computer system capable of answering questions posed in natural language, developed in IBM's DeepQA project by a research team led by principal investigator David Ferrucci. Watson was named after IBM's founder and first CEO, Thomas J. Watson.

Watson, the computer system, started with amazing achievements, and at least initially there seemed to be no limit to potential insights. However, by 2018, problematic results could not be ignored. Watson algorithms were capable of generating incorrect cancer treatment recommendations. Critics contend that Watson is using old-style expert knowledge to drive learning. Expert knowledge may work when the rules are both known and not changing, such as in a game of chess, but in medicine any "rules" are partial and can be constantly changing.

Why is using data streams of short, episodic clinic and hospital encounters insufficient to generate meaningful (business-relevant) predictive insights of complex systems? Three key reasons jump to mind:

- Pre- and post-conditions are too different, too quickly
- High-yield data elements are missing
- Logic is not enough

PRE- AND POST-CONDITIONS ARE TOO DIFFERENT, TOO QUICKLY

Here we pull from a non-healthcare scenario, but one that many are familiar with. Most grocery stores today do not invest in on-site excess inventory. Extra items do not generate revenue and are considered a cost center. Better instead to fill shelves with items and refill on demand as customers purchase them. Grocery loyalty cards track items at checkout for these retail chains and feed requirements for on-demand purchase orders to restock the shelves.

This works well when yesterday's customers behave the same way as today's customers. But when behavior changes on a dime across an entire customer base, standard AI has no way of predicting or preventing massive disruption of stock availability. Empty shelves are bad for business.

At the height of COVID-19, grocery store shelves were frequently empty. We can blame the disease for reducing the available workforce to ship and stock items on shelves. The winter weather also had an impact on transport trucks. Perhaps most importantly, customer behavior flipped in ways that eluded AI management.

Take coffee, for example. Before the pandemic, many of us used a coffee shop for the vast majority of our consumption and rarely brewed a cup at home. With COVID-19-inspired home offices, we flipped our behavior almost overnight. Suddenly, a once-in-a-quarter purchase of coffee beans needed to happen weekly, and no one warned the grocery store's AI.

Life is messy. Pre- and post-conditions in complex systems can change on a dime. Just because we understood yesterday does not mean we're able to predict tomorrow.

HIGH-YIELD DATA ELEMENTS ARE MISSING

GE wouldn't manage jet engine performance with a fifteen-minute data-gathering episode separated by weeks, months, or years. Tesla can design for massive data connectivity to the mothership and uses these continuous streams to advance self-driving capabilities. Machines are easy to interrogate using sensor-rich technologies. Humans are less straightforward.

George Gilder's *Life after Google: The Fall of Big Data and the Rise of the Blockchain Economy* reminds us that, by design, AI is based on logic.[83] Yet logic is not a universal theory, as not all things can be proven by reason alone. A systems biology speaker once shared this example, which relates to AI-enabled drug-discovery processes.

We are discovering drugs in silico today. This means rather than extracting substances from plants and testing their effectiveness in petri dishes in a lab, we instead build models of expected biological targets on computer chips. Then we run a stream of digital therapeutic candidates past these targets in order to predict which of the candidates may exhibit preferred behavior in real life.

Imagine that we need a drug to enter the nucleus of a cell in order to deliver the needed therapeutic result, such as vaccine-mediated immunity. Experts can design a digital model of a nuclear port (our biological doorway into the nucleus of our cells, where we store our DNA). Using this model, hundreds and thousands of potential digital candidates could be screened using AI for possible use in vaccine development.

These models have practical limitations. The yellow fever vaccine, available since 1937, predates computers and AI but remains one of our most effective vaccines. Allow me to repeat: this vaccine confers meaningful immunity across populations.

Imagine the surprise when the AI screening model of a yellow fever vaccine resulted in rejection! The AI kicked it out as unlikely to be effective. Clearly, designing models based on three-dimensional configurations and surface charges, plus a few other parameters, is woefully insufficient to explain the in vivo (in real life) experience confirming the efficacy of the yellow fever vaccine. If electrical charge logic and three dimensions is not enough, what would many multiple dimensions look like, and how could we get there?

These are not small problems. An IBM Watson timeline indicates that after years of effort and various successes, by 2018 the tide had turned. The algorithm could, in some cases, recommend "potentially harmful treatments."[84]

AI-based models need more data, better data, and more timely data than medical encounters, imaging, laboratory testing, and wearables-basically more than web2 approaches currently provide. How do we solve these issues?

At its core, the solution enables an ownership economy complete with financially incentivized, ongoing, and permissioned high-yield data streams direct from complex free-living systems.

Most importantly, we rely on the continuous creativity of human health expression across crowds to self-correct algorithms.

Indeed, web3-supported new business models are proving to be the basis of our next inflection of extreme value creation. Crypto may be an early use case, but the edges of healthcare are also taking advantage of blockchain, cryptography, and tokenized incentives. In doing so, businesses advance beyond the extractive behaviors of web2 platforms and partner with customers to co-produce health intelligence at the pace of change.

Will using AI actually help nudge health behaviors to be safe? This brings up a host of questions that loom large within the scientific community. Max Tegmark's book *Life 3.0: Being Human in the Age of Artificial Intelligence*, which I cited earlier, is a remarkable resource.

If AI is capable of recursive self-improvement, will humans lose control? Tegmark states that technology is neither good nor bad. It is just a tool that can be used for either. How do we ensure technologies such as AI cannot be used against us?

First, let's not make the mistake of assuming that we only need to worry once we reach an advanced stage of AI. Even very unsophisticated—in other words, *dumb*—AI has already been shown to harm humans. The simple attention-optimizing AI of social media was able to learn quickly that emotionally charged content would keep us glued to our phones. It didn't matter if the content was true or not. Less truthful yet more emotionally charged content was even more effective at achieving the AI goal of keeping many eyes on screens for as long as possible.

Ask the same AI to do any other task and it will fail miserably, as it was designed to perform only one task: optimize the time spent glued to the screen.

An AI that only does one thing is clearly not close to the ultimate AI machine. We may be decades away from a time when machines outperform humans in most tasks. This is the point in movies where the machines take control. But the relationship between humans and machines need not be one of adversaries. Parents are more intelligent than young children, and their relationship flourishes because their goals are aligned. We can use this metaphor for our preferred human-machine relationship.

Tegmark explains that a safe or friendly AI depends on aligning human goals with machine goals. This would require three main conditions: the AI must understand our goals, it must adopt our goals, and it must retain our goals over time. Making this happen is an unsolved problem and the subject of research. It will not be enough to simply align human goals with AI; all other powerful structures must also have shared values: democracies, corporations, countries, and so on. This problem will need thinking from computer scientists, political scientists, economists, ethicists, mathematicians, and more. Can we get it done? The need is ever more urgent.

Sadly, the funding for safe AI research is a tiny fraction of the funding to build more powerful AI. This bears resemblance to the funding for prevention in health. Prevention funding is a tiny fraction of the funds directed toward treatment. Treatments, regardless of their clinical effectiveness, tend to generate reliable business models. How do you pay for something that was prevented? After all, it didn't happen.

Humanity is facing a host of compelling questions in our modern, technologically advancing environments. Hopefully we can get them right most of the time. To this end, Tegmark and Elon Musk have launched a grant program for AI safety research. Ensuring AI safety, if achieved, will benefit all industries, including healthcare.

CHAPTER ELEVEN

BEYOND PUSHBACK, WHO ARE OUR EARLY ADOPTERS?

For anything to start in earnest, the system will need early adopters—those who bridge the gap between niche areas (gaming, for instance) and a more robust type of universal use. Ideally, such early adopters will care about their health on a fundamental level. In fact, the state of their health expression and physical performance—aiming for optimal—may even be tied to their professional endeavors.

What follows are two use cases meant to help draw a picture of an early adopter. Both individuals are athletes. The first, Terrell, lives and competes along the web2 healthcare rails, while the second, Jayson, does the same within the web3 health architecture.

TERRELL (WEB2)

When he was eight years old, Terrell's father told him he would eventually either have to excel in sports or get a job to help support the family. There would be no negotiation. Even to his young ears, this didn't quite sound reasonable, but luckily, Terrell was always the biggest kid in his class. As a teen, he reached six feet, three inches and 220 pounds, which set him up for football, basketball, and baseball. He became the "hero child," doing well in sports and in academics, and also taking care of his younger siblings.

His scholastic achievement helped him garner extra attention and support from his teachers, and Terrell was on track to go to college with a full ride. Though he preferred baseball, he couldn't imagine toiling in the minor leagues during his late teens and early twenties without a guarantee of making it to MLB. Division I football, on the other hand, felt like a surer bet.

Recruitment was an all-encompassing experience for Terrell and his family. Coaches reached out, and collegiate offers soon began to roll in. As a young man who had always been one of the bigger players on the field, Terrell hadn't yet experienced too much of the physical toll of playing football. In fact, he'd never sustained a major injury—only basic soreness the day after a game.

Terrell's talents on the field and in the classroom landed him at a school that was known for its scholar-athletes as well as its championship potential. But like most players, Terrell's career would soon include injury. The first came during his freshman season, when he suffered a minor knee injury that impacted his anterior cruciate and anterior collateral ligament. Team doctors concluded that surgery was not necessary, so he received physical therapy and a workout regimen that might strengthen his muscles to further stabilize his knee.

More minor injuries followed, but Terrell was able to finish his four years and enter the NFL. Throughout his early and mid twenties, as Terrell worked to establish himself as a consistent contributor, his body continued to fall into various levels of disrepair.

Many players learn quickly that injuries carry a curse. The business side of the sport demands fully functioning machines, not just warm bodies. Players mask injuries as best they can, while others work their way back with slim hope of a second chance.

Terrell lost a full year recovering from injuries to his knee and his shoulder. He was just shy of twenty-seven when his NFL career finally ended, Terrell having only played a handful of downs, mainly on special teams.

No one told Terrell that even though his career was short, his life expectancy would drop by as many as ten years, if not more. Meanwhile, his ability to walk would be impaired by the time he reached his late thirties, if not sooner. And, considering the constant head-to-head contact he endured as a middle linebacker and special teams player, brain health could very well become an issue over time.

Would Terrell have changed his decision to pursue football instead of baseball if he'd had more access to correlative insight? It's hard to say. Given his family and social situation and his desire to complete a degree and fast-track to the pros, he may have still decided on football.

Even when evidence points to unwelcome outcomes, many people, Terrell included, like to assume that things will be different. We'll be the outlier, the exception, the one who avoids injuries and climbs to the top of our sport. And if injured, we'll have a full recovery. Just believe enough and it will happen, goes the promise.

Regardless of what degree of unrealistic optimism we harbor, without access to data and correlative insight, what option do we have but to hope while doing our best to plan? In web2, while there are plenty of stories of injured players, we lack the detailed data package that might point the way where specific injuries are concerned. In our current state, we do not possess information symmetry, and families do not know what teams know. However, if more information were to become available to us, and if the playing field for this insight were to level off, then we would have a responsibility to collect this new knowledge and put it to use for the greater good.

JAYSON (WEB3)

Jayson is blessed with good genes. Along with his tall stature, he is talented in sports, learning and quickly perfecting new skills with seemingly little effort. His parents played soccer and volleyball, so they were very supportive of advancing his talents while careful to avoid overexposure that might put their son at risk of physical injury or the widespread threat of burnout.

Born in the web3 future, Jayson receives his SSI at birth. His parents manage it, and over time, various segments increasingly drop into Jayson's control. The family and Jayson use a range of wearables, apps, and games to manage and enhance his longitudinal health record. They know that getting into the best schools and onto the best teams requires a dossier of details... at age five, ten, twelve, and so on. He charts his three-mile race times, nutritional history samples, dexterity ranges, and injury details, along with a bevy of team- and sport-specific data (positions played, goals scored, etc.). At eighteen, Jayson takes on full custodianship of his information.

The advantages to tracking early childhood metrics beyond the basics include the opportunity to port these into data unions or commons that collect similar data from children across the globe. Soccer stars in the UK, Sweden, and Australia all mix the details of their daily lives so simple correlation AI can highlight the co-occurrences that may be associated with the best outcomes: specific meditation the night before big games, best uniform materials, meal choices for endurance in excess heat, and warm-up exercises other teams may not have thought of.

Jayson's parents engage in a share-to-earn model. They authorize various correlations to be served up to Zone III and benefit from fees or tokens associated with these transactions. Tokens act as discount cards for merchandise, game tickets, travel vouchers, and more. The family uses a personal fiduciary AI to help locate the best options for value returned in exchange for data elements. They simply specify the types of purchasers and use cases they are willing to provide data to. They wrap Jayson's data segments using zero-knowledge proofs and NFTs in order to monetize them via various marketplaces.

Phone-use data and media views remain in high demand. Whenever the family is looking for extra cash, they set the defaults such that data flows to one purchaser between 3 and 7 p.m., then switches over to another from 8 to 11 p.m. for a few weeks. The other common way to earn passive income includes keeping the family's devices on and powering various blockchain networks overnight.

During practice one day, Jayson suffers a dreaded anterior cruciate tear. He shares his medical images and clinical assessment across the injury data union or commons and gains detailed recommendations regarding presurgical prep, surgical repairs, and postsurgical rehab based on tens of thousands of other players that have worked their way back from a similar injury. The family analyzes cost and outcome data and has direct insight into choosing the best options for treatment, surgery, and physical therapy.

From there, they even enlist a service to mint tokens to begin preparing for Jayson's future income (in sports or academics). These services have a built-in personal fiduciary to ensure Jayson's best interests are not compromised in favor of generating greater returns to token holders.

These final two use cases are quite different, though both involve young athletes. Terrell's story brings Troy from Part I to mind; much like Troy and his parents were in the dark as it related to various health choices, young athletes and their families have little option to provide informed consent to participate in activities that carry the risk of significant harm. Shoshana Zuboff, Harvard professor and author of several books, including *The Age of Surveillance Capitalism: The Fight for a Human Future at the New Frontier of Power*, said, "There is no autonomous judgment without awareness." We are arguing for information symmetry or full—or at least reasonable—awareness.

Would access to the digitized health experience of previous players help new players avoid injury, as well as recovering from injury more effectively? Clearly this could be the case. But who wants this? Teams typically have a bench filled with talented players hoping to get time on the field. Rip and replace may be the operative motto here. Team managers rely on age and injury to ensure players exit in a timely manner. Younger, stronger, faster players can easily be jettisoned in to fill the slot.

Of course, leveraging web3 tools would provide players with safe and secure methods to generate and share a detailed digital version of their personal health journeys. Parents, coaches, and athletes themselves may be active customers of a marketplace offering relevant and certified health experiences. There is unquestionable value in rendering the once unknowable known.

Leagues may not be incentivized to make transparent any health details of the game. Their goals are not entirely aligned as winning may be a predominant goal. However, though players clearly want to win, they also want to live. To live long, functional, predominantly pain-free lives with brain function fully intact. Slightly misaligned goals can be difficult to detect, let alone correct.

Was the interval of fame and fortune worth the mobility and emotional toll? Would transparency into player life span and healthspan impact the pool of potential players? Is there a significant asymmetry between what leagues know about us and what we know about them? The world can be a rough place.

Early on in their journeys, children are too young to provide informed consent, so the adults in the room need to do their best to align goals at every stage of development. We have a responsibility to provide youngsters with solidly relevant truths, and knowing a lot more would be helpful.

How will our youth have access to all that is reasonably knowable? What does it look like when our data power asymmetry is repaired? If we are to be free—truly free—individuals, then we have a responsibility to ensure what is reasonably known is, in fact, known. Coming back to Shoshana Zuboff once more, "we won't fix any societal problem, ever, unless we reclaim the sanctity of information integrity and trustworthy communications." If it is to our advantage to digitize and quantify our health expression, then it must be on our own terms.

CHAPTER TWELVE

WHY NOW?

To put it simply, our timing might just be ideal. Life's complexities continue to accelerate at an alarming pace. COVID-19 launched an unprecedented level of an immediate human need for knowledge. This desire powered collaboration and value creation around the globe. In just months, the scientific community had sequenced the offending virus, understood which viral surface elements might be the best to target, and had begun generating a number of effective vaccines.

Clearly many decades of research underpinned our mechanistic understanding of infectious disease and enabled such rapid progression. By now, research and tech have helped streamline our ability to target viral diseases: impact the virus, and by default you impact the illness.

For decades, pharmaceutical companies have built robust business models dependent on a single molecule that can reliably impact disease. This one-target drug approach may be reaching its limit. The one-target options seem to be exceedingly rare, and multi-specific targets can take decades to sort out, hence the race to manage diverse human complexity. Can the three-zone model I introduced in Part III of this book provide access to the level of complexity management that industry requires? What would industry pay for this access? Will new data practices provide a steady stream of real-world data to help rapidly convert once undruggable targets into druggable ones?

What will become of Long COVID-19, for example? The manifestations are so varied that a single target is unlikely. What are the concrete elements that measure something of relevance in the clinical pathway? Where do we start? We need targets for new therapeutics, but finding these elements of relevance is not straightforward.

Take a neurodegenerative disease such as Parkinson's; we simply lack good surrogate markers. Markers are a way of easily measuring the presence and severity of a disease. In an ideal world, we would have good markers we could measure in the blood, tears, or saliva, but with Parkinson's, researchers depend on the *patient diary* as a marker of disease.

Patients or family members report progressing symptoms, such as slow movements, tremor, apathy, and depression—all suggesting a potential progression of disease. Sadly, by the time we're building patient diaries, disease processes are often well underway. What were the daily co-occurrences that predated disease onset? Would it be possible to accumulate enough understanding of relevant clusters of markers to catch Parkinson's before it is even perceptible by the patient? Stop it in its tracks? What constitutes resilience? How could it be measured? Be enhanced?

These questions are even more important when time is of the essence, which is why I chose to focus the book's first use case on Troy and the sensitive setting of puberty. It's also why I chose to focus on Truun later in the book. Children living with obesity during these years may be subject to profound alterations of their academic, vocational, and social potential. This all occurs at a time when they are too young to offer informed consent.

Troy deserved better. His cohort and parents lacked access to the type of information that Truun's cohort and parents, living in the web3 future, will ideally possess.

In that same future, it's my hope that the web3 architecture will allow us to manage our personal health expressions for our own benefit, as well as the benefit of others. We can imagine any number of data unions surfacing to aggregate databases designed to answer specific questions: What incentive structures work with subcategories of youth? Which COVID-19 vaccine combinations are most effective for which cohorts? Women versus men? Youth versus older adults?

Questions such as these highlight the nature in which our lives have become even more interdependent with the lives of others. Nothing short of a crowd will be able to teach us what matters when it comes to complexities such as Long COVID-19, youth incentive mechanisms, and more.

Today, teams are already building solutions that provide for nimble learning environments using web3 approaches. Consider the emerging *metaverse*, for instance. In the most simplistic terms, the metaverse is a three-dimensional enhancement of web3, like a spatial web. It includes the cultural ethos of partici-pants, who own and manage personal assets inside a powerfully enhanced three-dimensional immersive experience.

HEALTHCARE IN THE METAVERSE

What does the metaverse, or something similar, look like in healthcare? Transitioning ideas into practical scenarios can be difficult. However, we can explore a solution called QSTN, an ecosystem where users answer questions, earn credits, and spend these rewards within a digital environment built on the NEAR protocol. We'll examine it with the help of one last use case, a young person named Raylee, with the pronouns they/them.

Raylee has gathered almost 2000 $ANSR credits. Like many young adults across the globe, they log in to the QSTN app every day, answer only five questions, and get to watch their cred-its climb. In the meantime, Raylee's QSTN app shares all sorts of interesting insights. Yesterday, in a couple of minutes, they tapped out their answers, including the fact that Raylee prefers salty snacks over sweets. The app shared with them that 3,471 people answered this question, and those who preferred salty snacks tend to enjoy a significantly more optimistic personality than their sweet snack colleagues.

Raylee uses their $ANSR credits to purchase in-app assets and experiences within the QSTN metaverse. They especially appre-ciate that education is subsidized within the metaverse college. Their three-dimensional classroom is filled with diverse class-mates from around the globe, and these students bring a lot of amazing firsthand experience to the class. In just another nine weeks, Raylee will be fully certified in trauma-focused cognitive behavioral therapy (TF-CBT). Their metaverse waiting room has already gathered a forty-seven-person waiting list, as therapists with this training are increasingly in demand.

This scenario is just one example of what happens when you financially reward people for doing something as simple as answering five questions per day. As a result, you help create a high-fidelity understanding of on-the-ground conditions as well as their correlations to human outcomes. This type of information is invaluable for healthcare and other industries.

Social determinants of health drive the greatest amount of health expression. Our almost $3 trillion industry increasingly understands that hospitals and clinics encounter data that remain insufficient to optimize business intelligence, as the industry moves from fee-for-service to value-based reimbursement. This is already underway, as hospitals are penalized for readmissions within a thirty-day window of discharge.

There is a huge challenge with value-based reimbursement. For instance, while physicians may adhere to evidence-based guidelines in managing their diverse patient rosters, the outcomes can be significantly off target. Typically, these reasons are not easily uncovered. Why, for instance, would diabetic teens seem to chronically have laboratory tests indicating that their medical management was not effective? What is going on?

Solutions such as QSTN could craft a series of questions over a several-week period. A number of key trends might emerge.

Many teens today are in and out of health coverage. In some cases, this means that they are sharing insulin prescriptions with friends. This results in there not being enough insulin to go around, and hence poor laboratory test results. Critically, this may never come up via typical interactions with the healthcare system, nor would it be recorded in physician notes.

Some teens are especially generous with sharing their prescriptions. By chronically under-injecting insulin, these teens achieve a much-desired side effect: weight loss. Keeping weight off ensures that a pair of cool jeans in a smaller size will indeed fit!

Teens not able to access TF-CBT may be struggling with intermittent self-loathing and thoughts of self-harm, further complicating their willingness to comply with optimal self-care.

Balancing the influence of the social determinants of health with the delivery of evidence-based care cannot be done with encounter or clinic data alone. Encounter data can verify that the health system's quality metrics have not been met. In a value-based reimbursement model, this can negatively impact financials in a robust manner.

Therefore, modern health systems need to understand the ebb and flow of factors outside of the limits of the clinic or hospital. QSTN can safely and effectively provide the on-the-ground high-fidelity understanding, which powers health systems in avoidance of hefty financial penalties.

Why does QSTN work? At its core, QSTN exists to give individuals power and control over their data. Clearly, data has become a human rights issue, and empowering end users has become increasingly feasible via the tools available through web3 approaches.

Web2 and web3 have made relevant an entire new vocabulary: data labor, data leverage, conscious data contributions, and more. Nick Vincent and his team have generated a useful framework for these and other terms.[85] Innovators support the notion that web3 tools are especially suited to address the problems these terms define.

When Raylee chooses to answer questions, they are engaging in data labor and conscious data contributions, with the knowledge that their identity and data will be protected. In addition, the data they help generate will only be used for those purposes for which they have provided an approval.

QSTN does not engage in data labor theft. QSTN rewards conscious data contributions with tokens: $ANSR credits. Raylee can use or hold these credits to achieve outcomes they seek within the platform (college credits), as well as other goods outside the platform (via exchanges).

QSTN safely and effectively incentivizes collaboration between companies and consumers by providing a sustainable data economy through leveling the playing field. Rather than the gross data asymmetry of web2 applications, web3 participants can expect to personally manage their data to achieve both health and economic benefits.

In other words, the aim is a truly positive-sum ecosystem, where participants receive immediate value for their contributions and have the agency to choose to contribute to causes they support. In this way, communities can safely generate the health intelligence needed to ensure the best outcomes for progress, people, and the planet.

Time for a quick wrap-up.

CONCLUSION

Today each of us expects to have control over our own destinies, but navigating our personal futures requires being able to see a sufficient distance around the corners. It means having the tools to collaborate in projects that matter.

There have never been as many options. Our navigating complexity increases with each technological advance, and we can no longer afford to decide blindly because the options for failure are abundant.

Rugged individualism is a myth. We are interdependent, and without access to those that went before, we're on standby hoping that the medical-industrial complex will be there to rescue us from our missteps and hopefully do us no harm in the process.

Meanwhile, healthcare has been touting patient-centric transformation for decades. Until now, the tech stacks supporting this vision were seemingly unavailable. Now, however, a web3 ownership economy is illuminating a new direction. Many are intrigued with the possibilities, and we can be confident that computers need not control us; they can be instruments of freedom, protection, and personal agency.

Artists and musicians are paving a new way forward. These highly talented individuals used to be dependent upon galleries and record labels to determine their worth and forge relationships with their fan base. Now NFTs make it possible for individual artists and musicians to manage the distribution of their own work and reap the financial benefits, plus design and deliver effective reward systems to their customers directly.

A similar model in healthcare has recently launched. It is transforming the researcher-and-patient relationship and involves intellectual property NFTs, known as IPNFTs. Here's how they work.

Large pharmaceutical companies used to vertically integrate the development of new drugs; they did it all, from discovery to testing to commercialization. This is a notably expensive proposition, especially when most drug candidates do not make it through the entire process. Traditional IP structures forced companies to avoid collaborating and instead hide discoveries from each other. In short, biotech is devoid of effective incentive mechanisms to collaborate and, as a result, achieves too little, too slowly, and for too great a cost.

To save time and money, these companies look to academic centers to discover promising drug targets and early candidates for these targets. Once the academic work moves over to the drug companies, the original inventors, like artists and musicians, have little control over follow-on events. Pre-patent legal agreements between academia and industry can be difficult, slow, and again, expensive.

Furthermore, many promising therapies may not meet the blockbuster criterion or otherwise lack sufficient return on investment (ROI), stipulated by industry. When profit potential determines what gets done, promising innovations with lower ROI are abandoned. We need better, more innovative, and flexible business models. This is another opportunity for new governance approaches and token-based economics.

Imagine a group of like-minded individuals that share a common diagnosis. They join forces in the form of a DAO for the expressed purpose of developing new therapies. They secure a number of potential candidates from academia using IPNFTs. They collaborate on findings in a transparent manner, and for the first time, professionals and patients are working side by side to co-produce a preferred tomorrow.

This is happening today. It is all part of a blossoming decentralized science (DeSci) movement, which is optimizing talent, collaboration, and funding strategies by linking participants within an ownership economy.[86] Within this movement, new core infrastructure is operationalizing the vision: Molecule is a decentralized modular drug development solution in two parts (drug candidate discovery and finance).[87] They worked with VitaDAO to transfer IPNFTs and fund research focused on longevity. Others doing this work include PsyDAO and LabDAO.

The opportunities are growing daily. If we're to participate on our own terms, we must be able to own and manage our personal data. This should be a basic human right, and the technical infrastructure to support this right should be available, just as the infrastructure that ensures clean drinking water is a human right.

Given the tools to participate, we imagine millions of citizens collaborating across common goals. Younger generations are embracing new models. Almost 44 percent of men under thirty own a crypto wallet.[88] These tokens can provide new incentives and drive engagement across diverse populations in the co-creation of personally relevant health intelligence.

This knowledge tsunami would usher in the next wave of wealth creation, but getting the data right may be the easy part. Getting the AI right is likely the bigger challenge here.

No doubt there is much to learn, and we'll need a lot of learners. Gone are the days we can remain on standby waiting for scientific discoveries to save the day. The days are coming too quickly, with too much complexity, to leave it up to the few. The tools, the incentives, and the tasks are lining up for each of us to participate. Hopefully this narrative has provided you with a useful starter pack of concepts and use cases to begin your own web3 and ownership economy journey.

If you're brand new to these topics, seek out basic podcasts and webinars generated by respected experts, such as those found on Coinbase Learn. Here you will find simple visuals that explain: What is blockchain? What is Ethereum? What is crypto? And so on. Other options include sessions that literally instruct your path forward: "What to watch, read, and stream." If you gravitate to tech narratives, *Wired* magazine has a highly readable explainer, "What Is Blockchain? The Complete Wired Guide." Should you prefer to attend a quick online class, I recommend Arry Yu's Crypto Fundamentals, registered on the Maven platform.

Assuming the basics are part of your daily discourse, head to the *Ownership Economy* podcast, "the podcast that explores the people and ideas that are utilizing technology, economics, and the law to reimagine how the economy can work for everyone. Here we connect with the entrepreneurs, investors, thought-leaders, academics, and politicians that are constructing a better economy, one based on broad-based ownership and democratic governance. Hosted by Martin Smith and Jahed Momand, two investors and operators that aim to use this platform to showcase the people and ideas that will shape more inclusive economies."[89]

Bidirectional learning matters. Don't simply ingest ideas presented by others; repurpose them in conversation, tweets, posts, and debates with as many people as will listen. Road test assumptions, and seek out the naysayers.

We cannot afford to remain on standby, expecting others to deliver our preferred future—this is too important to let slide. Humanity is facing its most perilous moment in evolution to date. The systems we have in place today were built on our watch, and we alone have the responsibility to provide alternative rails for the future.

Will we succeed in regaining access to our full genetic potential? Will we render the attributes of outlier health knowable by all? Will we build sustainable AI that nurtures and protects humans? Today technology remains agnostic, and the future is not deterministic. It relies on our deliberate design. May you find, join, and share in educating crowds of enthusiastic individuals insistent on pulling up their sleeves and contributing to a prosperous and intelligence-rich future built on personal data economies.

The time to get started is now.

RESOURCES

Below is a short list of books that have informed the ideas in these pages and may aid in your bidirectional learning.

1. *Life after Google: The Fall of Big Data and Rise of the Block-chain Economy* by George Gilder
2. *Life 3.0: Being Human in the Age of Artificial Intelligence* by Max Tegmark
3. *Sapiens: A Brief History of Humankind* by Yuval Noah Harari
4. *The Age of Surveillance Capitalism: The Fight for a Human Future at the New Frontier of Power* by Shoshana Zuboff
5. *The Bitcoin Standard: The Decentralized Alternative to Central Banking* by Saifedean Ammous
6. *Superintelligence: Paths, Dangers, Strategies* by Nick Bostrom
7. *The Fourth Industrial Revolution* by Klaus Schwab
8. *Broken, Bankrupt, and Dying: How to Solve the Great American Healthcare Rip-Off* by Brad Spellberg
9. *Everybody Lies: Big Data, New Data, and What the Internet Can Tell Us about Who We Really Are* by Seth Stephens-Davidowitz

ABOUT THE AUTHOR

DR. BRIGITTE PINIEWSKI is a rare balance of medical, technical, and innovation expertise, with a true talent for explaining complex topics in ways that help others see why they matter. After many years as a primary care physician with obstetrics, she became chief medical officer for one of the largest reference laboratories in the Pacific Northwest. Here, she led collaborations with international universities and health technology alliances to advance population health innovation. Dr. Piniewski is now a subject matter expert for investor health tech diligence, as well as a startup advisor for teams leveraging blockchain and web3-based solutions. *Wealthcare: Demystifying Web3 and the Rise of Personal Data Economies* is her first book.

ACKNOWLEDGMENTS

This narrative has been many years in the making. As clinicians, we recognize our medical school education is but a framework from which to begin to comprehend the vast expression of human health that would confront us in the clinic and hospital. This education seed then relies on a steady trove of patients to advance our knowledge by considering diverse contributors specific to their health experience. This daily flood of specifics further fine-tunes and challenges previous assumptions. We owe our patients a lot. I am hopeful that by not letting their health experience remain silent or simply evaporate into thin air, I have begun to repay a debt. Patients trust our profession with their most delicate data. They deserve better.

Immediately in setting out to acknowledge those that contributed, panic rises, knowing that surely I will have missed mentioning someone, perhaps multiple people worthy of noting. This narrative benefits from speaking directly with thoughtful, curious intellectuals from a wide array of disciplines. It has been a genuine privilege to learn from them.

Many have patiently helped shape my thinking over extended discussions, including Adrian Gropper, CTO of Patient Privacy Rights and principal at HIE of One; Richard Whitt, founder of Deeper Edge LLC and president of GLIA Foundation; Arry Yu, chair of the US Blockchain Coalition (WTIA); James Marzolf, MD, senior director, health sector finance and policy, at the Whole Health Institute; Jim St. Claire, Transformation of Outcomes in Public Health and Linux Foundation Public Health; and Jeff Gaus, founder and CEO of the Provenance Chain Network.

Others include John Macaulay, Daniel McMorris, Johannes Ernst, Chris Ingrao, Wilf Penfold, Dane Stout, Steve Brown, Theban Ganesh, Kyle Bergquist, John MacDonald, Rafael Mojden, Mary Carbajal, Omid Moghadam, Michael Fitzgerald, Teage Christensen, Travis James, Tess Gadwa, Alek Tan, Joshua Tan, Ned Saleh, Nick Ellingson, Stefan Renton, Marcus Estes, Adie Rae, Orrin Campbell, Ed Young, Tammie Arnold, David Ulbricht, Mardell Chinberg, Betsabe Botaitis, Marc Blinder, Rick Meider, David Kil, and Ran Whitehead.

Special thanks to Dave Jarecki, professional writer and storyteller, for his patient willingness to listen, critique, and edit my endless and often less organized stream of short narratives. With Dave's help, segments were arranged in a logical sequence and concepts became accessible to a wider audience.

I am excited to include the NEAR Foundation among the list of material contributors to this work. This foundation provided a Public Goods Grant to help cover publishing costs.

That brings me to the behemoth job of publishing. Thank you to all the Scribe Media folks who ensured professional quality was delivered at every turn. Miles Rote recognized potential for a book considering web3 from a healthcare lens. Then Libby Allen, Liz Green, Darnah Mercieca, Ami Hendrickson, Kathleen McIntosh, and others went to work to polish and package this complex narrative for easy consumption. Thank you all!

My sincere apologies to everyone else who ought to be remembered here.

Finally, a deep note of gratitude belongs to family and friends. You are my most valued distraction from the unnatural solitude of thinking and writing.

REFERENCES

1   Azeen Ghorayshi, "Puberty Starts Earlier than It Used To. No One Knows Why," *New York Times*, May 19, 2022, https://www.nytimes.com/2022/05/19/science/early-puberty-medical-reason.html.

2   Nick Lavars, "World-First Study Links Childhood Obesity to Lower Cognition in Midlife," New Atlas, June 16, 2022, https://newatlas.com/medical/world-first-study-childhood-obesity-lower-cognition-midlife/.

3   Berkeley Lovelace Jr., "Aetna CEO: Warren Buffet's 'Tapeworm' Analogy Fits—Health-Care Costs Squeeze the Economy for Trillions," CNBC, March 26, 2018, https://www.cnbc.com/2018/03/26/aetna-ceo-buffetts-tapeworm-analogy-fits-health-costs-hurt-economy.html.

4   Steve Finlay, "GM Is Getting Sick of High Health-Care Costs," WardsAuto, March 1, 2004, https://www.wardsauto.com/news-analysis/gm-getting-sick-high-health-care-costs.

5   Eric Topol, *The Creative Destruction of Medicine: How the Digital Revolution Will Create Better Health Care* (New York: Basic Books, 2012).

6   Robin G. Nelson, "How a Virus Exposed the Myth of Rugged Individualism," *Scientific American*, March 1, 2022, https://www.scientificamerican.com/article/how-a-virus-exposed-the-myth-of-rugged-individualism/.

7   Shoshana Zuboff, *The Age of Surveillance Capitalism: The Fight for a Human Future at the New Frontier of Power* (New York: Public Affairs, 2019).

8   *The Social Dilemma*, directed by Jeff Orlowski-Yang (Exposure Labs and Argent Pictures, 2020), Netflix.

9   Tom Simonite, "When It Comes to Health Care, AI Has a Long Way to Go," *Wired*, January 16, 2022, https://www.wired.com/story/health-care-ai-long-way-to-go/; "What Is Federated Learning?" Google Cloud Tech, February 5, 2021, YouTube video, 5:35, https://www.youtube.com/watch?v=X8YYWunttOY.

10   Simonite, "When It Comes to Health Care."

11   Yuval Noah Harari, "Why Technology Favors Tyranny," *Atlantic*, October 2018, https://www.theatlantic.com/magazine/archive/2018/10/yuval-noah-harari-technology-tyranny/568330/.

12   Sebastian Herrera and David Benoit, "Why the Amazon, JPMorgan, Berkshire Venture Collapsed: 'Health Care was Too Big a Problem,'" *Wall Street Journal*, January 7, 2021, https://www.wsj.com/articles/why-the-amazon-jpmorgan-berkshire-venture-collapsed-health-care-was-too-big-a-problem-11610039485.

13   George Gilder, *Life after Google: The Fall of Big Data and the Rise of the Blockchain Economy* (Washington, DC: Regnery Gateway, 2018).

14   Brigitte Piniewski, "Is Cannabis to Healthcare as Bitcoin Is to Finance?" LinkedIn, February 2, 2022, https://www.linkedin.com/pulse/cannabis-healthcare-bitcoin-finance-brigitte-piniewski-md/?trackingId=s6WSFqQ%2BQzqEB2nPn6Fnpg%3D%3D.

15   Shermin Voshmgir, "Web3, Blockchain, Cryptocurrency: A Threat or an Opportunity?" TEDx Talks, December 20, 2018, YouTube video, 17:57, https://www.youtube.com/watch?v=JPGNvKy6DTA.

16   "Welcome to the Semantic Mining of Activity, Social, and Health Data Project (SMASH)," SMASH, 2013, http://aimlab.cs.uoregon.edu/SMASH/.

17   Clay Shirky, *Here Comes Everybody: The Power of Organizing Without Organizations* (New York: Penguin Press, 2008).

18   Arry Yu, "The Blockchain Super Glossary," Cascadia Blockchain Council (WTIA), 2018, https://docs.google.com/document/d/1Vdwa4R_XXhSQFU7ELXheT55FyWorwZXbSWRYjYGetqA/edit#heading=h.4a509bua04ay.

19   Matthew Spoke, "Blockchains and the Ownership Economy," *Forbes*, October 27, 2020, https://www.forbes.com/sites/mattspoke/2020/10/27/blockchains-and-the-ownership-economy/?sh=7ff906673d0d.

20   Jeff Wilser, "Self-Sovereign Identity Explained," CoinDesk, October 1, 2020, https://www.coindesk.com/policy/2020/10/01/self-sovereign-identity-explained/.

21   Don Tapscott and Alex Tapscott, "What Blockchain Could Mean for Your Health Data," *Harvard Business Review*, June 12, 2020, https://hbr.org/2020/06/what-blockchain-could-mean-for-your-health-data.

22   Satoshi Nakamoto, "Bitcoin: A Peer-to-Peer Electronic Cash System," 2008, https://bitcoin.org/bitcoin.pdf.

23   "Welcome to Ethereum," Ethereum, updated September 15, 2022, https://ethereum.org/en/.

24   Micah Zoltu et al., "Introduction to Smart Contracts," Ethereum, August 25, 2022, https://ethereum.org/en/developers/docs/smart-contracts/#top.

25 "Cryptocurrency Prices by Market Cap," CoinGecko, accessed September 22, 2022, https://www. coingecko.com/?locale=en&page=1.

26 Saifedean Ammous, *The Bitcoin Standard: The Decentralized Alternative to Central Banking* (Hoboken, NJ: Wiley, 2018).

27 Max Read, "Why Your Group Chat Could Be Worth Millions," Intelligencer, *New York Magazine*, October 24, 2021, https://nymag.com/intelligencer/2021/10/whats-a-dao-why-your-group-chat-could-be-worth-millions.html?fbclid=IwAR0FkWMZPBrOS7FimV3frZqciUED2yL3SfeEnBurkPe6Hd9nWxCzr2FVlgs.

28 "What Is Federated Learning?" Google Cloud Tech.

29 Mona Flores, "Triaging COVID-19 Patients: 20 Hospitals in 20 Days Build AI Model That Predicts Oxygen Needs," *Nvidia* (blog), October 5, 2020, https://blogs.nvidia.com/blog/2020/10/05/federated-learning-covid-oxygen-needs/.

30 Jaakko Tuomilehto et al., "Prevention of Type 2 Diabetes Mellitus by Changes in Lifestyle among Subjects with Impaired Glucose Tolerance," *New England Journal of Medicine* 344, no. 18 (May 2001): 1343–50, https://doi.org/10.1056/nejm200105033441801; Michel de Lorgeril et al., "Mediterranean Dietary Pattern in a Randomized Trial: Prolonged Survival and Possible Reduced Cancer Rate," *Archives of Internal Medicine* 158, no. 11 (June 1998): 1181–87, https://doi.org/10.1001/archinte.158.11.1181; Meir J. Stampfer et al., "Primary Prevention of Coronary Heart Disease in Women Through Diet and Lifestyle," *New England Journal of Medicine* 343, no. 1 (July 2000): 16–22, https://doi.org/10.1056/nejm200007063430103; Frank B. Hu et al., "Diet, Lifestyle, and the Risk of Type 2 Diabetes Mellitus in Women," *New England Journal of Medicine* 345, no. 11 (September 2001): 790–97, https://doi.org/10.1056/nejmoa010492; Kim T. B. Knoops et al., "Mediterranean Diet, Lifestyle Factors, and 10-Year Mortality in Elderly European Men and Women: The HALE Project," *JAMA* 292, no. 12 (September 2004): 1433–39, https://doi.org/10.1001/jama.292.12.1433; Rainer Hambrecht et al., "Percutaneous Coronary Angioplasty Compared with Exercise Training in Patients with Stable Coronary Artery Disease: A Randomized Trial," *Circulation* 109, no. 11 (March 2004): 1371–78, https://doi.org/10.1161/01.cir.0000121360.31954.1f; Michel de Lorgeril et al., "Mediterranean Diet, Traditional Risk Factors, and the Rate of Cardiovascular Complications after Myocardial Infarction: Final Report of the Lyon Diet Heart Study," *Circulation* 99, no. 6 (February 1999): 779–85, https://doi.org/10.1161/01.cir.99.6.779; Ram B. Singh et al., "Randomised Controlled Trial of Cardioprotective Diet in Patients with Recent Acute Myocardial Infarction: Results of One Year Follow Up," *BMJ* 304, no. 6833 (April 1992): 1015–19, https://doi.org/10.1136%2Fbmj.304.6833.1015; Ram B. Singh et al., "Effect of an Indo-Mediterranean Diet on Progression of Coronary Artery Disease in High Risk Patients (Indo-Mediterranean Diet Heart Study): A Randomised Single-Blind Trial," *Lancet* 360, no. 9344 (November 2002): 1455–61, https://doi.org/10.1016/s0140-6736(02)11472-3; Roberto Marchioli et al., "Early Protection Against Sudden Death by n-3 Polyunsaturated Fatty Acides After Myocardial Infarction," *Circulation* 105, no. 16 (2002): 1893–1903, https://doi.org/10.1161/01.CIR.0000014682.14181.F2.

31 Xiaoliang Ling et al., "Model Ensemble for Click Prediction in Bing Search Ads," *WWW '17 Companion: Proceedings of the 26th International Conference on World Wide Web Companion* (April 2017): 689–98, https://doi.org/10.1145/3041021.3054192.

32 Jeff Desjardins, "How the Tech Giants Make Their Billions," Visual Capitalist, March 29, 2019, https://www.visualcapitalist.com/how-tech-giants-make-billions/.

33   Gilder, *Life After Google.*

34   Max Tegmark, *Life 3.0: Being Human in the Age of Artificial Intelligence* (New York: Alfred A. Knopf, 2017).

35   Susan Wile Schwarz and Jason Peterson, "Adolescent Obesity in the United States: Facts for Policymakers," National Center for Children in Poverty, November 2010, http://www.nccp.org/publication/ adolescent-obesity-in-the-united-states-facts-for-policymakers/.

36   Izzuddin M. Aris et al., "Analysis of Early-Life Growth and Age at Pubertal Onset in US Children," *JAMA Network Open* 5, no. 2 (February 4, 2022): e2146873, https://doi. org/10.1001%2Fjamanetworkopen.2021.46873.

37   "Obesity and Overweight," fact sheet, World Health Organization, June 9, 2021, https://www.who.int/ news-room/fact-sheets/detail/obesity-and-overweight.

38   Matt Berger, "Children Worldwide Aren't Getting Enough Exercise—Here's What We Can Do about It," Healthline, November 20, 2019, https://www.healthline.com/health-news/ children-around-the-world-dont-get-enough-exercise.

39   "Obesity Consequences: The High Cost of Excess Weight," Harvard T. H. Chan School of Public Health, accessed September 22, 2022, https://www.hsph.harvard.edu/obesity-prevention-source/obesity-consequences/; Edvard Johansson, Urpo Kiiskinen, and Markku Heliövaara, "The Effect of Obesity on Wages and Employment: The Difference between Having a High BMI and Being Fat," *Hanken School of Economics Working Papers* 528 (June 13, 2007), https://econpapers.repec.org/paper/hhbhanken/0528.htm; Kjetil A. van der Wel, "Long-Term Effects of Poor Health on Employment: The Significance of Life Stage and Educational Level," *Sociology of Health and Wellness* 33, no. 7 (November 2011): 1096–111, https://doi. org/10.1111/j.1467-9566.2011.01346.x.

40   Ghorayshi, "Puberty Starts Earlier than It Used To."

41   "Hereditary Breast Cancer and BRCA Genes," Centers for Disease Control and Prevention, last reviewed September 27, 2021, https://www.cdc.gov/cancer/breast/young_women/bringyourbrave/hereditary_ breast_cancer/index.htm.

42   Rachel Modarelli et al., "Pediatric Diabetes on the Rise: Trends in Incident Diabetes during the COVID-19 Pandemic," *Journal of the Endocrine Society* 6, no. 4 (April 2022), https://doi.org/10.1210/jendso/ bvac024.

43   Paul B. Ginsburg and Steven M. Lieberman, "Medicare Payment for Physician-Administered (Part B) Drugs: The Interim Final Rule and a Better Way Forward," USC-Brookings Schaeffer on Health Policy, February 10, 2021, https://www.brookings.edu/blog/usc-brookings-schaeffer-on-health-policy/2021/02/10/ medicare-payment-for-physician-administered-part-b-drugs.

44   Harari, "Why Technology Favors Tyranny."

45   Alex Mashinsky, "AMA with Arry Yu and Guest Alex Mashinsky," *Windshield Time*, July 27, 2021, YouTube video, 59:58, https://www.youtube.com/watch?v=XCKG7Y5GFfw.

46   Zirui Song and Katherine Baicker, "Effect of a Workplace Wellness Program on Employee Health and Economic Outcomes: A Randomized Clinical Trial," *JAMA* 321, no. 15 (April 16, 2019): 1491–501, https://doi.org/10.1001/jama.2019.3307.

47   Robert H. Shmerling, "How Long Will My Hip or Knee Replacement Last?" *Harvard Health Blog*, Harvard Health Publishing, March 29, 2021, https://www.health.harvard.edu/blog/how-long-will-my-hip-or-knee-replacement-last-2018071914272.

48   Scott Galloway, "Prime Health," *No Mercy / No Malice* (blog), July 29, 2022, https://www.profgalloway.com/prime-health/.

49   "Physical Activity for Different Groups," Centers for Disease Control and Prevention, last reviewed July 29, 2021, https://www.cdc.gov/physicalactivity/basics/age-chart.html.

50   "About Us," BurstIQ, accessed September 22, 2022, https://burstiq.com/company/.

51   Glenn Hubbard, "Even My Business-School Students Have Doubts about Capitalism," *Atlantic*, January 2, 2022, https://www.theatlantic.com/ideas/archive/2022/01/mba-students-against-capitalism/621117/.

52   S. Jay Olshansky et al., "A Potential Decline in Life Expectancy in the United States in the 21st Century," *New England Journal of Medicine* 352, no. 11 (March 17, 2005): 1138–45, https://doi.org/10.1056/nejmsro43743.

53   Mike Roth, "A Letter to Web3 Builders," Medium, December 9, 2021, https://mikeroth.medium.com/a-letter-to-web3-builders-ca97ce7f98d1.

54   Richard Whitt, "To Fix the Web, Give It Back to the Users," *Fast Company*, January 22, 2019, https://www.fastcompany.com/90293980/to-fix-the-web-give-it-back-to-the-users.

55   Nick Vincent, "Should Tech Companies Be Paying Us for Our Data?—With Nick Vincent," interview by Jed Tabernero and Shikher Bhandary, *Things Have Changed*, podcast, 32:11, November 1, 2021, https://www.thc-pod.com/episode/should-tech-companies-be-paying-us-for-our-data-with-nicholas-vincent.

56   Nicholas Vincent et al., "Data Leverage: A Framework for Empowering the Public in Its Relationship with Technology Companies," *FAccT '21: Proceedings of the 2021 ACM Conference on Fairness, Accountability and Transparency* (March 2021): 215–27, https://doi.org/10.1145/3442188.3445885.

57   Makena Kelly, "Andrew Yang Is Pushing Big Tech to Pay Users for Data," The Verge, June 22, 2020, https://www.theverge.com/2020/6/22/21298919/andrew-yang-big-tech-data-dividend-project-facebook-google-ubi.

58   Deflationary token, burn to ensure appreciation of the asset and offset selling pressure from the use of funds for unexpected costs.

59   RVRS, *Reverse Whitepaper: Activating Communities Worldwide*, accessed September 22, 2022, https://reverseclimatechange.com/wp-content/uploads/2022/02/WHITEPAPER20FRONT-combined.pdf. The bulleted list above is loosely based on the framework of this white paper.

60 Adrian Gropper, LinkedIn profile, accessed September 22, 2022, https://www.linkedin.com/in/adrian-gropper-6916651/.

61 Zuboff, *The Age of Surveillance Capitalism.*

62 Adam Tanner, *Our Bodies, Our Data: How Companies Make Billions Selling Our Medical Records* (Boston: Beacon Press, 2017).

63 Security.org Team, "47 States Have Weak or Nonexistent Consumer Data Privacy Laws," Security.org, April 14, 2020, https://www.security.org/resources/digital-privacy-legislation-by-state/.

64 Andrew Perrin and Sara Atske, "7% of Americans Don't Use the Internet. Who Are They?" Pew Research Center, April 2, 2021, https://www.pewresearch.org/fact-tank/2021/04/02/7-of-americans-dont-use-the-internet-who-are-they/.

65 Katherine J. Wu, "Will Omicron Leave Most of Us Immune?" *The Atlantic*, January 21, 2022, https://www.theatlantic.com/health/archive/2022/01/omicron-wave-immunity/621324/?utm_source=newsletter&utm_medium=email&utm_campaign=atlantic-daily-newsletter&utm_content=20220124&utm_term=The%20Atlantic%20Daily.

66 Jay Stanley, "Identity Crisis: What Digital Driver's Licenses Could Mean for Privacy, Equity, and Freedom," ACLU, May 2021, https://www.aclu.org/report/identity-crisis-what-digital-drivers-licenses-could-mean-privacy-equity-and-freedom.

67 Madeleine Armstrong, "Big Pharma Piles into Machine Learning, but What Will It Get Out of It?" Evaluate Vantage, July 31, 2018, https://www.evaluate.com/vantage/articles/analysis/vantage-points/big-pharma-piles-machine-learning-what-will-it-get-out-it.

68 "Why Do Patients Drop Out of Clinical Trials?" *mdgroup* (blog), October 2, 2020, https://mdgroup.com/blog/why-do-patients-drop-out-of-clinical-trials/.

69 Brian Kihoon Lee, "Deep Learning on Electronic Medical Records Is Doomed to Fail," *moderndescartes.com* (blog), March 22, 2022, https://www.moderndescartes.com/essays/deep_learning_emr/.

70 Kate Vitasek et al., "How Walmart Canada Uses Blockchain to Solve Supply-Chain Challenges," *Harvard Business Review*, January 5, 2022, https://hbr.org/2022/01/how-walmart-canada-uses-blockchain-to-solve-supply-chain-challenges.

71 "PLAY-TO-EARN | 30 Second Trailer," PLAY-TO-EARN, May 11, 2021, YouTube video, 0:30, https://www.youtube.com/watch?v=cQZroKpbWfc.

72 Jesse Walden, "Past, Present, Future: From Co-Ops to Cryptonetworks," Variant, March 22, 2019, https://variant.fund/articles/past-present-future-from-co-ops-to-cryptonetworks/.

73 Klaus Schwab and Peter Vanham, "What Is the Difference between Stakeholder Capitalism, Shareholder Capitalism and State Capitalism?" World Economic Forum, January 26, 2021, https://www.weforum.org/agenda/2021/01/what-is-the-difference-between-stakeholder-capitalism-shareholder-capitalism-and-state-capitalism-davos-agenda-2021/.

74 Gilad Edelman, "The Father of Web3 Wants You to Trust Less," *Wired,* November 29, 2021, https://www.wired.com/story/web3-gavin-wood-interview/.

75 Forrest Briscoe et al., "Evolving Public Views on the Value of One's DNA and Expectations for Genomic Database Governance: Results from a National Survey," *PLoS One* 15, no. 3 (March 11, 2020): e0229044, https://doi.org/10.1371/journal.pone.0229044.

76 Jason Prado, "Episode 006—Worker Ownership and the Future of the 'Gig Economy' with Jason Prado of the Driver's Cooperative," interview by Martin Smith and Jahed Momand, *The Ownership Economy,* podcast, 55:17, March 11, 2022, https://anchor.fm/theownershipeconomy/episodes/Episode-006---Worker-Ownership-and-the-future-of-the-Gig-Economy-with-Jason-Prado-of-the-Drivers-Cooperative-e1ff3no.

77 Adrian Gropper, "A Human Rights Approach to Personal Information Technology," *Bill of Health* (blog), April 12, 2022, https://blog.petrieflom.law.harvard.edu/2022/04/12/a-human-rights-approach-to-personal-information-technology/#more-30847.

78 Joshua Tan, "Episode 010—Modeling Digital Community Governance with Joshua Tan of the Metagovernance Project," interview by Martin Smith and Jahed Momand, *The Ownership Economy,* podcast, 51:25, April 8, 2022, https://anchor.fm/theownershipeconomy/episodes/Episode-010---Modeling-Digital-Community-Governance-with-Joshua-Tan-of-The-Metagovernance-Project-e1grpgp.

79 E. Glen Weyl, Puja Ohlhaver, and Vitalik Buterin, "Decentralized Society: Finding Web3's Soul," *SSRN* (May 11, 2022), http://dx.doi.org/10.2139/ssrn.4105763.

80 Weyl, Ohlhaver, and Buterin, "Decentralized Society."

81 David S. Ludwig et al., "The Carbohydrate-Insulin Model: A Physiological Perspective on the Obesity Pandemic," *American Journal of Clinical Nutrition* 114, no. 6 (September 13, 2021): 1873–85, https://doi.org/10.1093/ajcn/nqab270.

82 ATCC, "Six Factors Affecting Reproducibility in Life Science and How to Handle Them," Nature Portfolio, https://www.nature.com/articles/d42473-019-00004-y.

83 Gilder, *Life after Google.*

84 Elizabeth Cairns, "Watson, Watsoff," Evaluate Vantage, January 24, 2022, https://www.evaluate.com/vantage/articles/news/deals-snippets/watson-watsoff.

85 Vincent et al., "Data Leverage."

86 Tyler Golato, "The Emergence of Biotech DAOs," *Molecule* (blog), Medium, January 28, 2022, https://medium.com/molecule-blog/the-emergence-of-biotech-daos-407e31748cd4.

87 "What Is Molecule?" Molecule Documentation, last modified January 2022, https://docs.molecule.to/documentation/introduction/what-is-molecule.

88   Andrew Perrin, "16% of Americans Say They Have Ever Invested In, Traded or Used Cryptocurrency," Pew Research Center, November 11, 2021, https://www.pewresearch.org/fact-tank/2021/11/11/16-of-americans-say-they-have-ever-invested-in-traded-or-used-cryptocurrency/.

89   "Summary," *The Ownership Economy*, podcast, Audible, accessed September 23, 2022, https://www.audible.com/pd/The-Ownership-Economy-Podcast/B09XBJVQJS.

CPSIA information can be obtained
at www.ICGtesting.com
Printed in the USA
JSHW010805300123
36957JS00007B/8

9 781544 537719